POWERLIFTING
for beginners

The ultimate guide to training for and entering your first few competitions

by David Penney PhD, DSc

ISBN: 978-1-8381528-7-1

Published by SSP (Siri Scientific Press).

The author has made every effort to contact copyright holders of material reproduced in this book and people who appear in the photographs and is grateful for permissions granted. If any have been inadvertently overlooked, he apologises for the oversight, and hopes it will be accepted in good faith.

Image Credits

Lift Daly (LD): website no longer active
Flownamix (FMX): https://www.flownamix.co.uk
White Lights Media (WLM): https://whitelightsmedia.com

All other images provided by the author unless stated. The use of images in this project was discussed with the creators at the time of purchase, sometimes in person at the various competitions. Several attempts were made to contact all image creators in order to obtain written confirmation for image re-use in this book and the author is grateful to those who responded.

Attempts were also made to contact people who appear in the images, as a courtesy, to confirm that they were happy for their image(s) to appear in the book. The author is very grateful to Kim Cowell for facilitating this through confirming the identities of some of said individuals and the following are thanked for granting permission: Adam Anderson, Zahida Bibi, Dave Clifford, Bob Evans, Matt Fij, Florence Henriksen, Oliver Hexter, Chris Jennings, Pete Moore (for Ethan Moore), Clare Patterson, Steevi Pugh, Shakham Shakeri, Darren Stafford, James Williamson and Jacob Wymer. Other people, where identified, were contacted but did not reply.

Disclaimer: Because physical exercise can be strenuous and subject to risk of serious injury, the reader should obtain a physical examination from a doctor before embarking on any exercise activity, including those outlined in this book. Always consult a suitably qualified professional before beginning any nutritional or exercise program, or using any unfamiliar training equipment. Never disregard professional medical advice or delay in seeking it because of something you have read or experienced. The content of this book is for information and educational purposes only and any exercise programs started are done so entirely at your own risk and the author and his affiliates cannot be held responsible for any injuries incurred as a result. It is always advisable to train under the supervision of an experienced coach. The information contained in this book is not intended to be a substitute for professional medical advice, diagnosis or treatment in any manner. Always seek the advice of your physician or other qualified health provider with any questions you may have regarding any medical condition.

CONTENTS

Preface

As you enter the venue, the scent of sweat and iron fills your nostrils. The sound of death metal playing and barbells and steel plates clanking against the ground fills the air as you make your way to the seating area for the audience. As you walk by, you see men and women of all shapes and sizes, some with bulging muscles, others not, but all preparing to lift an incredible amount of weight on the platform that takes centre stage. It's an exciting and intimidating sight all at once.

There is a buzz in the air as the MC and the rest of the competition crew put all the final touches in place, and ready the platform to get the competition under way. The judges take their seats and the loaders add the weights to the bar ready for the first lift of the day. You can see a line of lifters waiting, pacing around, looking very focused, all of them 'in the zone'. The one at the front is chalking her hands and chomping at the bit, ready to get on the platform, but is prevented from doing so by a raised arm of one of the officials.

Eventually, the MC whips the crowd up into a frenzy ready to cheer on the first lifter of the day and announces that, "the bar is loaded" and the official lowers her arm to let the lifter access the platform. The crowd cheers her on as she storms up to the bar, steely eyed and sets up under it with power and passion. The platform spotter crew are there beside her but she does not notice them, such is her focus on the bar and the commands of the centre referee, which she follows with precision to execute a perfect opening squat to get the competition under way. "It's three white lights and a good lift", bellows out the MC. Within seconds the weights on the bar have been changed and the next lifter is called up to do the same as the crowd continues to cheer them on.

But what if I told you that at the next competition you could be one of the lifters?

This book will take you on a journey to discover the exciting world of competition powerlifting. Whether you're a complete beginner or someone who's been hitting the gym for a while, you'll learn everything you need to know to compete in this thrilling sport. Even if you are already a year or two in to powerlifting, you will still find plenty of useful information here.

It will cover the basics, including the three main lifts - squat, bench press, and deadlift – and give you tips and tricks to perfect your technique for training in preparation for executing all three lifts to competition standard on meet day.

You'll learn how to create a training program that works for you, and discover the mental toughness needed to push through your limits. You will also get an in-depth look at the world of competitive powerlifting, including what to expect on competition day, how to choose the right meet, and how to mentally and physically prepare yourself for the challenge ahead. A main aim of this book is to prepare you for your first few competitions, such that you avoid the myriad of potential newbie lifter mistakes, that so often result from an inadequate knowledge of what to expect on the day and can easily result in you bombing out (being disqualified) of the competition completely.

With the right mindset, training, and dedication, you'll be well on your way to becoming a powerlifting champion. So, what are you waiting for? Let's get started!

Powerlifting is suitable for most people and you are never too old to get started. Zahida Bibi is a 45-year-old mother of three young children, seen here getting some experience at a non-sanctioned 'club' competition, 2023. Six years ago Zahida visited the gym three times per week but would never have considered lifting weights. When she started she would never have entertained the idea of competing. Now she is a PT and trains other women, with a primary focus on barbell lifts. Image credit FMX.

What is Powerlifting?

Powerlifting is a competitive strength sport consisting of three different compound lifts: squat, bench press and deadlift, where competitors are grouped into different classes according to sex, age and bodyweight. As defined by the IPF (International Powerlifting Federation), the age classes are as follows:

Sub-junior: (18 years-old and under)
Junior: (19–23 years-old)
Open/Senior: (24–39 years-old)
Age category is dependent on the year of the participant's birth. For example, if the participant turns 18 years-old in January, he or she is still considered a Sub-junior until the end of that calendar year
Masters 1: (40–49 years-old)
Masters 2: (50–59 years-old)
Masters 3: (60–69 years-old)
Masters 4: (70+ years-old). A lifter becomes a Masters 1 on the 1st of January of the year that they turn 40 years-old. Some federations use 5-year increments, for example, 40–44, 45–49, 50–54, etc. and may also include a sub-master class from 33 (or 35) to 39 years-old

The weight classes are typically as follows:
Men: up to 53 kg (Sub-Junior/Junior), 59 kg, 66 kg, 74 kg, 83 kg, 93 kg, 105 kg, 120 kg, 120 kg+
Women: up to 43 kg (Sub-Junior/Junior), 47 kg, 52 kg, 57 kg, 63 kg, 69 kg, 76 kg, 84 kg, 84 kg+

More will be said about competitions later, but in brief, each competitor is allowed three attempts on each of the lifts in the order: squat, bench press, deadlift, and their competition total is calculated by summing up the highest numbers for each of the different lifts, assuming those lifts were executed correctly as defined by the competition rules. The ultimate aim of competitive powerlifting is to lift as much weight as possible. For each age group and weight class, the lifter with the highest total wins. In many meets, the lifter with the highest total relative to their weight class also wins. That is, the relative strength of all lifters is compared to determine the best overall lifter of the competition and awards are usually presented for the best overall male and female lifters. If two or more lifters achieve the same total, the lighter lifter is ranked above the heavier lifter.

Powerlifting tends to lurk in the background, overshadowed by Olympic lifting and bodybuilding. Nonetheless, the sport has increased significantly in popularity over recent years, especially so with females. For example, in 2012 British Powerlifting had 815 members, of which 154 were female (18.9%). By 2022, a decade later, the numbers had increased to 3273 members, of which 1070 were female (32.7%). At the 2023 British Bench Press Championships 73 (44.2%) of the 165 competitors were female. Of course, there are other powerlifting bodies, so the total number of lifters in the UK will be higher, but there is no reason to expect any significant difference in the increase of female competitors.

Also in recent years, powerlifting has become more popular among university students and has now been included in the British Universities & Colleges Sport (BUCS) program for 2022/23. Many universities now have their own clubs, with lifters competing in dedicated University Championships. In 2016 there was a total of 129 lifters at the British University Championships, and at the same event in 2019 the number had risen to 444. By 2022 the number of competitors was down to 303, no doubt still in catch-up mode following the COVID lockdowns. British Powerlifting has also started running varsity competitions pitting one university team directly against another (e.g. Southampton vs Portsmouth, 2023).

Powerlifting continues to grow and make progress on the World Stage. At the 2022 World Games held in Birmingham, USA, Larysa Soloviova (Ukraine) took part in the Opening Ceremony walk in, an honour only accorded to athletes who have been voted the greatest of all time! She had previously won Gold each time she had been to the World Games, 2005–2017 and secured a Bronze this time around. Also at this year's event, two powerlifters were given the accolade of Athlete of the Day: Volodymyr Rysyiev (Ukraine) and Agata Sitko (Poland). Great Britain was represented by Emma Goodwin, Ellie Steel and Tony Cliffe, with Tony bringing home a Bronze medal. This was the first medal for team GB at the World Games since 1993 when Rodney Hypolite took Silver. Tony not only secured a podium finish but also broke the British Bench, bench only and Total equipped records.

March 25, 2003 witnessed the long-awaited (2020 COVID lockdown-postponed) SBD Sheffield Powerlifting Championships, held at the Sheffield City Hall in front of a live audience of 2000 spectators, the largest in powerlifting history. There was also a live-feed online, which by the following morning had more than 180,000 views. Moreover, there was a record prize pot of £365,000 on offer for placing in the top 10 and for breaking existing world records. Twenty-four lifters (12 male and 12 female) came from as far away as Japan, New Zealand and USA to compete for the largest prize in powerlifting history and they pulled out all the stops to create an awe-inspiring spectacle in an electrifying atmosphere.

There were ups and downs, some very risky squat and bench attempts nearly resulting in a couple of the lifters bombing out of the competition, but fortunately they managed to nail their third attempts under what must have been an inordinate amount of pressure. In total, 39 records fell, with Evie Corrigan from New Zealand claiming the women's title with a new world record total of 460 kg in the 52 kg division and Jesus Olivares (USA) taking the men's title with an amazing new world record total of 1152.5 kg in the 120+ kg division. This was a truly remarkable event, stamping Britain's mark on the powerlifting world stage and promoting the sport to a broad audience.

Now is an exciting time to get into powerlifting and hopefully, after reading this book, you will add yourself to these statistics! Go on, why not give it a try? Even if you decide it isn't your thing (which is unlikely), you will not have wasted much time in learning how to execute the lifts. It is not technically demanding and the transition from general weight training in a gym to training for competitive powerlifting is very straightforward. As you do not need to have great athletic ability in order to do it, it is an excellent choice for anyone who would like to venture into entry level competitive sport. It will serve to give your training more meaning and consequently more focus. Given that new powerlifters make rapid progress early on it is very easy to get hooked on the sport and to derive a great deal of satisfaction from it. However, be under no illusion, although powerlifting can be learnt within a matter of hours, it can take a lifetime to master.

Who does it?

Anybody 14 years of age or older can compete in powerlifting, though you can of course start training much younger than that. There is no upper age limit and you often see lifters over the age of 60 (Masters 3) pulling impressive iron at competitions. The majority of lifters fall within the Open/Senior category (24–39 years-old), but the other categories below and above this are also well represented both in terms of membership numbers and competition participation.

Junior and Sub-Junior lifters

There are plenty of young lifters getting involved in powerlifting as observed via the Junior (under 23) and Sub-Junior (under 18) age classes. The youngest age at which a lifter can compete is 14-years-old as a Sub-Junior. The Junior and Sub-Junior Championships 2022 hosted 217 competitors, and the British Juniors Classic Powerlifting Championships in 2019 had 226 lifters. However, these figures provide a significant underestimation of the number of Junior and Sub-Junior lifters. Of 3277 British Powerlifting members signed up by 10 Feb, 2023, 1192 were Juniors and 253 were Sub-Juniors. It is great to see such a significant number of youngsters engaging with the sport and this bodes well for the future development of British talent on the world stage.

Previously, it was thought that lifting heavy weights at an early age would stunt growth in children. However, numerous research studies have demonstrated that this is not the case, though you will still hear it said. On the contrary, resistance training involving knowledgeable coaches, effective supervision and tailored programming provide multiple benefits in young lifters. These include increased strength, better cardio-vascular fitness, lower rates of other-sports-related injuries, increased bone density with decreased risk of fracture, higher self-esteem and interest in fitness. Assuming a young child has fully developed their gross motor skills (they are able to run, balance, hop, skip, throw, catch, jump) they will be able to safely embark on a suitable and supervised resistance training program. It is advisable to have a coach or physical therapist screen them for ability prior to getting started.

Encouraging the development of physical and mental fortitude in our children as they progress into adolescence can only be a good thing, especially in this day and age when the overall health and fitness of our young people is in decline due

Sub-Junior lifter Ethan Moore deadlifting 100 kg for his opener at the North West Masters Powerlifting Championships, 2022, which he followed with 112.5 kg for his third attempt and a new -53 kg bodyweight class North West record, breaking his previous record of 110 kg which he secured at his first (Novice) competition earlier that year. He has broken this record several times since and it now stands at 138 kg (2023), as he chases the British record. At 14 years-old, he is just getting started! Image credit FMX.

Masters 2 lifter David Clifford about to squat 230.5 kg as his third attempt at the North West Masters, 2021 for a new -93 kg bodyweight class North West record.

to sedentary lifestyles and poor food, exercise and other life choices. Of course, there will be potential risks if children are not coached correctly, so if you are considering training for yourself or somebody else in the young age group make sure you get a suitably qualified and experienced coach. If the child has any underlying medical conditions you will need to get clearance from their doctor that they are fit enough to embark on such a program before they get started.

Masters lifters

The Masters contingent of powerlifting includes lifters aged 40 and over, as follows: Masters 1 (40–49 years-old), Masters 2 (50–59 years-old), Masters 3 (60–69 years-old), Masters 4 (70+ years-old). A lifter becomes a Masters 1 on the 1st of January of the year that they turn 40-years-old, they become a Masters 2 on the 1st of January of the year that they turn 50-years-old and so on.

Many championship competitions take these age classes into consideration and there are also competitions especially for Masters lifters. You have no doubt heard it said many times that, "age is just a number!" and indeed, there are many exceptionally strong old men and women who lift and who are very competitive against lifters several decades their juniors. As I write this, Andy Rigby has just set a new bench press World Record in the Masters 3 (60–69 years-old) -105 kg category of 203.5 kg at the 2023 World Championships in South Africa.

It is difficult to determine the exact number of Masters lifters in British Powerlifting due to the way membership data are compiled and logged. However, a good estimate can be obtained from www.openipf.org ASSUMING that the majority of Masters that are signed up members actually compete, and this is not an unreasonable assumption. The following data were derived from the database for UK competitive Masters powerlifters over the years 2019 (pre-COVID lockdown) and 2021, 2022 (post lockdown).

Year	Masters 1	Masters 2	Masters 3	Masters 4	Total
2019	441	181	50	6	678
2020	COVID lockdowns				
2021	297	146	44	8	495
2022	386	195	45	8	634

It can be expected that some Masters lifters would have stopped training during the 2020 lockdowns and not returned to the sport afterwards and others may have taken some time to return. Hence, there is evidence of a short lag phase as the numbers return to pre-lockdown levels.

To give an idea of the spread of lifters, the results of the British Masters Classic Championships 2022 recorded 118 Masters competitors split as follows (with total ranges in parentheses): female: 29 M1 (280–497.5 kg), 29 M2 (252.5–450 kg), 6 M3 (217.5–317.5 kg), 1 M4 (63.5 kg – bench only); male: 23 M1 (462.5–772.5 kg), 19 M2 (467.5–730 kg), 8 M3 (414–595 kg), 3 M4 (407.5–542.5 kg). Of course, these total ranges are spread across all the different weight classes, but they nonetheless demonstrate that there are some very strong older folks out there. Three lifters bombed out of the competition, two on squats, the other on deadlifts. The British Championships competitions require a substantial qualifying total, so the standard of lifting will be high.

Divisional competitions will usually have fewer lifters and lower totals overall. For example the North West Masters Classic Championships 2022, recorded 16 Masters classic competitors, split as follows (with total ranges in parentheses): female: 4 M1 (257.5–355 kg), 4 M2 (260–427.5 kg), 1 M3 (197.5 kg); male: 2 M1 (602.5–620 kg), 4 M2 (412.5–610 kg), 1 M3 (447.5 kg).

As already mentioned, you join a specific Masters class on the 1st January of the year that you turn 40, 50, 60 or 70. However, you can actually qualify for a Masters competition in the next class up before this date. For example, a 39 year-old lifter could hit a QT for the Masters 1 class of the British Masters Championships in the year before he or she turns 40, so long as the QT is hit at a sanctioned competition following the preceding British Masters Championships (a QT can be achieved any time following the previous competition up until five weeks before the next one). Current National Champions can defend their title without qualification, but should they wish to compete at a different bodyweight they must make the QT for that bodyweight class. Qualification for bench press only competitions can be achieved using the bench press in a full-power, three-lift competition.

What are the health benefits for older lifters?

Of course, most forms of exercise will be considered good for the majority of people, but powerlifting is particularly beneficial for people in their forties and

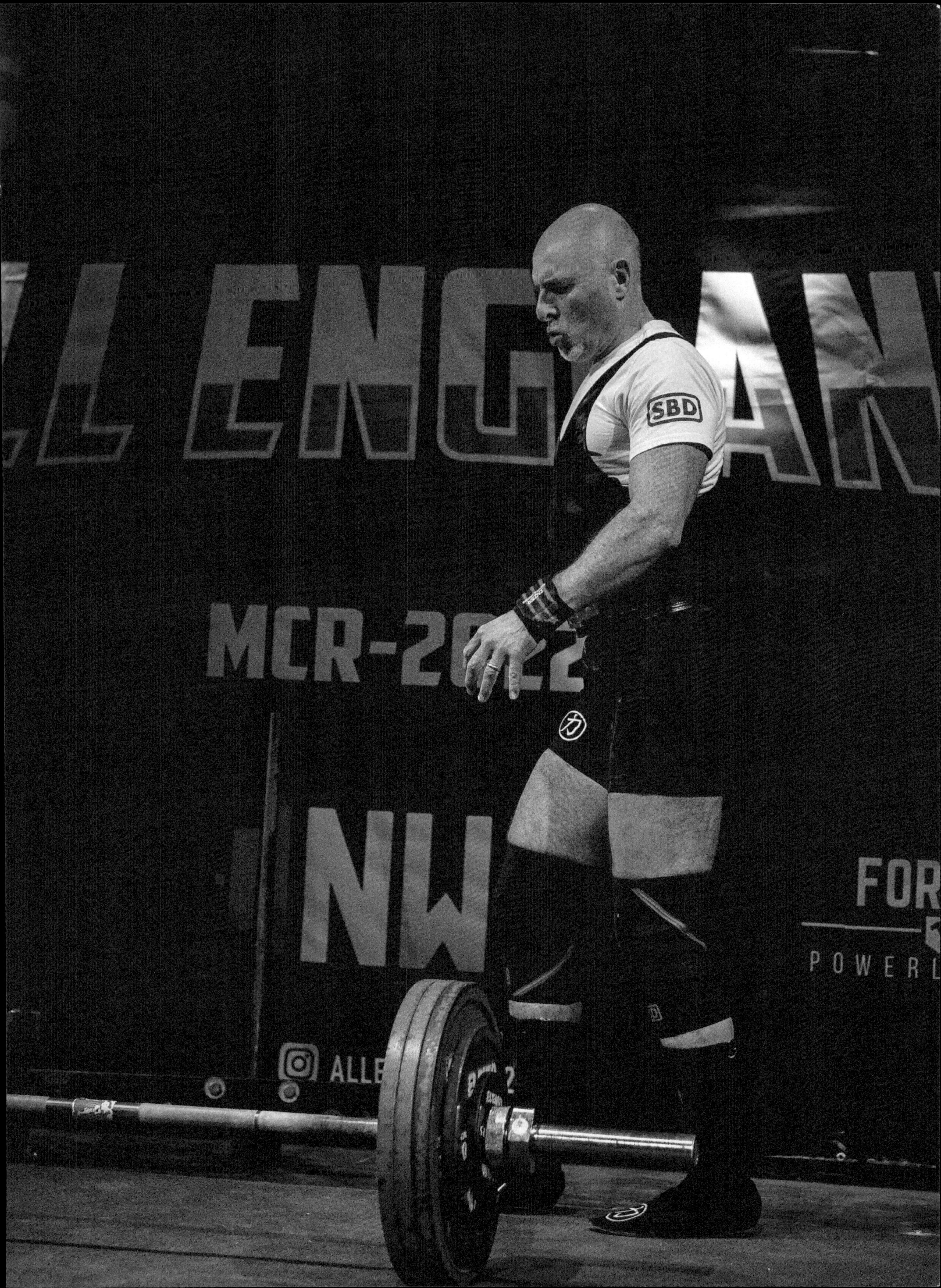
SBD
NW

beyond. This is because we lose muscle mass and strength as we age, especially so beyond the age of just 30-years-old, where it has been predicted that a normal adult will lose 3–5% of their muscle mass per decade, unless action is taken to prevent it. We also lose bone density as we age, commonly known as osteoporosis and the combination of these two elements (loss of muscle mass and bone density) makes us more prone (approximately 2.3 times) to hip and other fractures from falls, which are more likely as a result of reduced muscular strength and poor posture and stability.

As the old adage goes, *strength is never a weakness and weakness is never a strength*. There are few activities that being strong does not facilitate in one way or another and powerlifting will certainly make you much stronger, probably significantly stronger than in your youth, assuming you didn't previously do any serious strength training. Indeed, the three main compound lifts: squat, bench press and deadlift, when considered together, work just about every muscle in the body. All three can be considered full-body lifts when executed correctly. Even the bench press uses the core and lower body in the form of leg-drive as will be explained later.

Powerlifting is also beneficial for your cardiovascular system. Performing many repetitions with light weights really gets your heart pumping, so constitutes an excellent form of cardio (and is much more fun than plodding away on a treadmill). Indeed, if you are new to training it shouldn't be long before you notice a difference in normal daily activities becoming seemingly easier, whereas previously they may have left you somewhat breathless.

By reducing your body fat and increasing your lean muscle mass, your posture, flexibility and athleticism will improve. A good example of this relates to gardening, a pastime that many elder folks enjoy. After many winter months of doing very little, gardeners venture out in the early spring to start preparing their pots and flower beds for the better weather. This often involves extended periods in crouched or kneeling positions planting flowers, pulling up weeds, shifting heavy bags of fertilizer, turning over the topsoil with a fork and spade, etc. and can be quite exhausting for elderly people, leading to aching lower backs and other muscles for days afterwards. Such discomfort is unlikely to be experienced by those who train full-body compound lifts with heavy weights on a regular basis. The same goes for other activities which are only undertaken every now and then, but often involve putting the body in awkward positions that it is not used to, for example painting and decorating, unless of course that is your profession. And therein lies an additional point – this type of training can extend your working longevity also.

You will be able to maintain your independence and continue doing daily chores, which those around you of a similar age may start having difficulty with. Initially, these activities may be as simple as carrying shopping or walking up a flight of stairs – things we take for granted in our youth, but which the ravages of time will gradually strip away from us. As you progress with your training you will be able to handle more strenuous activities with ease, as per the gardening and decorating examples discussed above.

In addition to the functional issues, aging is a degenerative process marked by physiological and metabolic impairments, and diminished cognitive capacity. Those who start to take their training a little more seriously will soon realize that nutrition plays a key role in making decent and prolonged strength gains and as a consequence should start making better food choices. The combination of resistance training and better nutrition can prevent or even reverse metabolic syndrome, which is a group of health conditions that raise the risk of heart problems and type 2 diabetes.

A recent study in a group of elderly women demonstrated that regular resistance training provided significant gains in upper and lower body strength concomitant to positive improvements on cognitive capacities, resulting in enhanced quality of life. In short, you will be slowing down some of the normal aging processes. Moreover, an increasing amount of new research is demonstrating that you can actually **reverse** the effects of aging through strength training, even at the sub-cellular (e.g. gene) level.

Recent research has also shown that strength training can protect the parts of the brain vulnerable to Alzheimer's disease. Thus, Masters powerlifting is also likely to prevent or at least delay the onset of dementia.

Regardless of how old you are, it is never a bad idea to start making yourself as strong and fit as possible, for as long as possible. It is an investment that none of us can afford not to make! Make sure you check with your doctor to confirm you are healthy enough to do so (most people are!). Of course, many doctors are not particularly familiar with the methods and benefits of strength training, so may err on the side of caution in order to avoid potential legal consequences should you have an accident. You can always seek a second opinion.

Powerlifting tends to improve your life choices

Most forms of exercise are beneficial for the majority of people, but powerlifting has several unique features as touched on in the previous section.

Plenty of powerlifters appear to be overweight, some even morbidly obese, while others appear to be jacked, ripped or however else you may wish to describe somebody with a seriously muscular physique. Some overweight lifters are happy to remain like this, whereas others see powerlifting as a means to lose significant amounts of body fat or even increase bodyweight by adding lean muscle. Whatever your personal goals, they can be achieved so long as you train correctly and manage your nutrition accordingly and I have seen some remarkable weight loss stories involving powerlifting. Indeed, I am one of them.

Powerlifting training also has a significant cognitive element to it. The early stages of learning the lifting techniques requires a reasonable degree of mind/muscle/body co-ordination. Of course, so does subsequent training, but not to the same extent once the lifting techniques have been perfected. Working out training programs of sets, reps, assistance exercises, etc. (as will be discussed later) also takes some thought, especially when trying to break through a PB plateau or when preparing for a competition. Then of course there is the constant battle between mind and body as you strive to be better than you were the day/week/month/competition, etc. before. This requires constant focus and commitment, but is highly satisfying when significant goals are achieved. This may also transfer into additional motivation and confidence elsewhere in life.

Indeed, once you get bitten by the bug of powerlifting, you will find that you start to manage other elements of your lifestyle to further develop your strength potential. You will no doubt clean up your diet and calorie consumption, avoid excessive (or any) alcohol intake, quit smoking and other recreational drugs, and walk more rather than taking motorized transport. In short, your lifting prowess and strength development will inspire you to start making better and more healthy lifestyle choices, such that the benefits of progressing in the sport and evolving as a strength athlete will transcend far beyond your performance on the platform.

How safe is it?

There are always risks involved with any sport and powerlifting is no exception. Injuries can be defined in various ways, one being *an event that causes an interruption in training or competitions*. These injuries have been reported as relatively low frequency for powerlifters (1.0–4.4 injuries per 1000 training hours). However, injury can also be defined as *a condition of pain or impairment of bodily function that affects powerlifters' training*. Most of these injuries occur during training, although they rarely require the injured person to completely refrain from training (though they may change the content of training sessions), nor do they prevent powerlifters from competing.

The author competes under British Powerlifting as a member of the North West England division, pictured here at the British Bench Press Championships, 2020.

The lumbopelvic region, shoulder, and hip are the most commonly injured areas for both sexes. I have certainly tweaked all these regions during my powerlifting career and have even had a more serious injury consisting of a finger getting crushed under a 150 kg barbell and which was at risk of amputation. This happened in November 2019, just four weeks before a competition, which I still managed to attend, but didn't come away with any new personal bests (PBs) due to my reduced grip capabilities! Fortunately, the finger healed remarkably well and has had no further impact on my training. There is a full account of this on page 132.

You are likely at more significant risk of aches, pains, injury and illness if you don't engage in strength training. You will soon be able to tell the difference between muscle aches, which can be a natural result of training (e.g. delayed onset muscle soreness, or DOMS for short) and pains that are a result of injury. Most injuries occur while attempting new maximum lift PBs or as a result of poor lifting technique. Thus, the best way to avoid injuries is to make sure you learn the proper technique for each lift and to save PBs for the competition platform. Given that many injuries are due to overload, it is also very important to warm-up to your heavy work sets, rather than just diving straight in at the top end. If you do get injured, DO NOT try and train through it as you will only make matters worse, but you can of course train around it until your body heals itself and you can get back on with normal training again.

I hope none of this has put you off the idea of powerlifting. As mentioned earlier, the injury risk in powerlifting is relatively low compared to other sports (1.0–4.4 injuries per 1000 training hours). For example, some comparable data for other popular sports include: soccer (35 injuries per 1000 training hours), squash (18 injuries per 1000 training hours), netball (14 injuries per 1000 training hours), running (12 injuries per 1000 training hours) and tennis (5 injuries per 1000 training hours).

Powerlifting federations in the UK

There are several federations in the UK that cater to British powerlifters under a range of different circumstances and they often have different rules, weight classes, etc. A brief summary of the larger federations follows with website links for those who wish to delve deeper. Most federations will have a social media presence and regular AGMs. It is worth following them online to keep abreast of new changes to the technical rule book and the list of approved equipment suppliers, in addition to upcoming competitions and becoming a part of the powerlifting community.

British Powerlifting (htttps://www.britishpowerlifting.org/)

British Powerlifting (BP) was formed in 2008 from the powerlifting section of the British Weightlifters Association, which had been the original governing body of powerlifting in the UK since the inception of the sport in the 1950s. BP is the trading name of GB Powerlifting Federation Limited (GBPF) and is now (as of 2022) the Sports Councils' recognized National Governing Body for UK Powerlifting, excluding Paralympic Powerlifting (Bench Press). It is the largest powerlifting organization in the UK and the only one to have a fully WADA compliant Anti-Doping Programme, both in and out of competition and independently administered by the IPF.

GBPF is affiliated to the International Powerlifting Federation (IPF) and the European Powerlifting Federation (EPF) and comprises the Home Countries of England, Wales, Scotland and Northern Ireland. England is further split into the following ten geographic divisions: Yorkshire & North East, North West, North Midlands, West Midlands, East Midlands, Greater London, South West, South Midlands, South East and the recently added Manx (Isle of Man) division. Each division has its own independent calendar of regional events, where qualifying totals can be achieved for BP national competitions.

BP runs both assisted and "classic" (raw lifting) competitions. Tight knee sleeves and wrist wraps are permitted but knee wraps are not allowed.

British Drug-Free Powerlifting Association (https://www.bdfpa.co.uk/)

The British Drug Free Powerlifting Association is the trading name of Drug Free Powerlifting Ltd. and was originally formed in 1989. It aimed to provide an alternative national platform for drug free competition at a time when the use of performance enhancing drugs (PEDs) was rife and unchecked. All BDFPA events take place against the background of the association's unequivocal commitment to a policy of rigorous drug control. Tests are conducted at the Kings College London WADA Laboratory. Test refusals or anabolic positives normally result in an automatic life ban, subject to appeal.

As testament to their commitment to combating drugs in sport, they are the only Powerlifting federation recognized and affiliated to The Army, Navy and Royal Air Force Powerlifting Associations. The BDFPA is affiliated to the WDFPF (World Drug Free Powerlifting Federation), and is the only UK powerlifting organization recognized by the international body.

Global Powerlifting Committee GB (https://www.gpcgb.com/)

The GPC-GB was formed in 2008 for British lifters who wanted to compete in GPC international competitions. All aspects of lifting are catered for from Raw to Equipped plus single lifts, with competitions (catering for novices to world champions) held across the country ranging from the south, midlands and north of England and in to Wales, Scotland, Ireland and Northern Ireland. In recent years GPC-GB have had some great international success at GPC European & World Championships. According to the committee, the number of British lifters wanting to lift in the GPC-GB increases year on year, with more and more wanting to represent Team GB in GPC International competitions.

British Powerlifting Union (http://britishpowerliftingunion.co.uk/)

Formed in 2013, the British Powerlifting Union (BPU) took over the UK's affiliation to the World Powerlifting Congress (WPC) from the British Powerlifting Congress (BPC). It has different classes for raw lifting (with knee wraps [classic] and without – knee sleeves are not permitted). They also have different classes for equipped lifting (single or multiply). The BPU does not test for drugs, but the ABPU (Amateur British Powerlifting Union) has a targeted testing policy. The ABPU and the BPU are separate federations, both commercially and constitutionally, but are run together at competitions on the same platform.

Para Powerlifting (www.WorldParaPowerlifting.org)

Para Powerlifting for disabled lifters is open to athletes with cerebral palsy, spinal cord injuries, lower limb amputees and others who meet the minimal physical disability criteria. Following its debut as weightlifting in the Tokyo 1964 Paralympic Games, para powerlifting (as it has been referred to since the 1992 Barcelona Paralympics), has expanded from solely male athletes with spinal cord injuries to currently including male and female competitors with physical impairments that affect their lower limbs or hips and athletes with short stature. For more information on lifting with disabilities visit: www.WorldParaPowerlifting.org (the official website of World Para Powerlifting).

Open Powerlifting (https://www.openpowerlifting.org)

Open Powerlifting is a website database resource containing entries for more than 432,400 lifters globally. This community service project aims to create, update and maintain a permanent and open archive of the world's powerlifting data published to the Public Domain for access and use by anybody. These data include competition results, competitions entered and all associated data for each competitor. The database is fully searchable and can be filtered by geographical region, federation, drug-tested vs. non-tested, gender, weight class, age, year of competition, etc. It is a very handy resource for checking out your competition or seeing where you fall in the grand scheme of things. It is also useful for self motivation – it is always nice to see yourself move up in the listings each time you hit a new competition total PB. There is also an IPF specific frontend at (https://www.openipf.org) which includes around 13,300 UK based IPF lifters over all years for which records are included.

Performing the Three Lifts Correctly

This chapter concerns how to execute each of the three competition lifts: squat, bench press and deadlift with proper form. It is absolutely imperative that you learn the correct lifting technique at the outset for both safety reasons and because if you use correct form, which is mostly based on the physical efficiency of shifting the bar, you will be able to lift heavier weights. This is simply because using sub-optimal technique will require you to compensate by applying additional force to move a given load, when compared to using the most efficient biomechanical form appropriate to your own anthropometry (the physical properties/dimensions of your body).

Gravity acts vertically, i.e. straight downwards and any force you need to use against any non-vertical force due to poor mechanics is simply wasted effort. Hence, for both the squat and deadlift you will be looking to achieve a vertical bar path – both upwards and downwards bar movements tracking along the straight line. However, this is not the case for the bench press as will be explained later.

This chapter is based mainly on lifting for training and covers the basic principles. Additional considerations are required when performing these lifts at competition and these are covered later, in the Competitive Powerlifting chapter. Nonetheless, as you read through this chapter and practice the lifts it is worth keeping in mind that **the ultimate aim of any powerlifter is to employ the most efficient biomechanical leverages in order to recruit the maximum amount of muscle to move the heaviest possible weight through the minimum range of motion for a single rep as defined and permitted in the rules of the sport.**

Do not make the mistake of thinking that lifting heavy iron is dangerous, bad for your back, your knees or beyond your capabilities. It isn't, so don't let your mind start playing tricks on you before you get started! Besides, heavy is a relative term. A 100 kg deadlift might be a maximum lift for one person, whereas for another it may be their light warm-up weight. For the purposes of training, what other people are lifting is not important. It does not even matter what weight you start with, even if it is an empty bar (20 kg). Indeed, many people start this way and for some even that may be too heavy. All that matters is that you continue to make progress via progressive overload by adding very slight weight increments each time (more on this later) and regardless of where you start you will be amazed at how good you start to feel in just a very short period of time.

All three lifts are classed as compound full-body lifts because, when done correctly, each one utilizes all of the major (and many of the minor) muscle groups. There is nothing intrinsically difficult about these lifts because, after all, they basically mimic everyday movements such as lifting a box off the floor, pushing something away from you, or squatting down to rest on your haunches. By comparison, consider the incredible range of equipment available in most gyms, which has been designed to isolate specific muscles or muscle groups. Here you are very rarely, if ever, replicating 'normal' body movements. To compound matters further, when using machines the trajectory of the weights that you move is entirely governed by the lever mechanics of the equipment, rather than allowing the mechanical leverage of your own relative limb lengths to determine the best course for the weight to follow.

Think about it. People differ tremendously in their body morphology – some are short, some are tall, some have relatively long torsos with short limbs, whereas others have relatively short torsos with long limbs … and with all combinations in between. The body mechanics with regard to the efficiency of movement of an object will differ accordingly. Following the most efficient mechanical trajectory can be achieved easily with a free barbell, which lacks any form of associated restrictions, but isolation machines have rather limited flexibility in terms of being able to cater effectively for a wide range of different body types.

Lifting relatively heavy weights on a barbell is also safer in terms of avoiding repetitive strain injuries such as tendonitis (e.g. tennis elbow), a very common and painful complaint experienced by many people who use isolation machines or dumbbells. There are two main reasons for such conditions. The first, as discussed above is because excessive strain is being placed on individual joints, such as the elbows, which are being forced to operate in a manner or specific range of motion to which the body is unaccustomed. Furthermore, it is often the case that people using these machines are prioritizing larger muscle growth over increased strength, so they work at a higher rep rate (e.g. 10 to 12 or more repetitions of a specific exercise in each set). Those who are strength training with a barbell normally operate in the three to six rep range, purely because it is too heavy to lift more than this most of the time. Clearly then, repetitive strain injury is much more likely in the former training group.

One thing common to all the lifts mentioned above is that they all require a significant element of core body support when done properly. This will be discussed in more depth later, but in simple terms, it refers to the fact that the entire body should be braced against the load, including those parts of the body that you may at first glance think have nothing to do with the actual lift itself. Of great importance is that you build up internal pressure in your abdomen and thorax because this helps to produce structural stability around your spine in addition to general stability. When you walk in a gym and watch people doing these lifts it is often difficult to tell whether or not they are actually doing this. In many cases they are not bracing properly because the vast majority of people do not understand how to do these lifts correctly. Once you do know how to do them using proper form you will be very surprised to see how many other people around you are using very poor technique indeed.

So, why bother with proper form if it is possible to get away with using bad technique? First, if you use a poor technique you increase your risk of injury. Even minor injuries, such as pulled muscles, can slow down your progress. Obviously, more serious injuries can have a significant impact on your training. Second, if you are using proper form it means your body mechanical leverage and the movement path of the barbell are optimal, meaning you will be able to shift heavier weights with greater ease.

The correct technique will be discussed for each lift under the appropriate heading. However, these will be only pointers. This book is not the place for a comprehensive explanation of the intricacies of each of the lifts concerned because there are far too many and some excellent books (and other resources) already exist. The latest edition of the book *Starting Strength* by Mark Rippetoe is highly recommended in this regard. Indeed, there are many books about powerlifting and weight training in general, which include descriptions of how to do the lifts prescribed here, but the number of pages allocated to these explanations varies tremendously, ranging from just a single page to 50 pages or more! Clearly, one page will not teach you how to do any of these lifts correctly, as will become evident in due course, whereas a 50-page description (as in *Starting Strength*) will be far too much to take on board, such that you get everything right the first time you try it. Nonetheless, the more useful information you have at your fingertips the better, and you can keep coming back to it in order to improve your technique as you progress.

It is vitally important that you get the correct techniques nailed down early on, because while you will get away with small errors using light weights, these will eventually transform into larger errors as the weights increase! This holds true not only for your long term progression, but also for individual training sessions, where you will be warming up with light weights and gradually increasing the loads until you reach your heavy work sets for that particular session. It can be easy to lose absolute focus on proper form when doing your light warm-up sets, but you need to be highly disciplined in this respect. It will help you detect problems and rectify them, which is obviously a lot easier to do with a light load than with a very heavy one!

Whenever you move a barbell you are competing against the gravitational force that wants to bring it back down to the ground. This operates vertically, that is, straight down without any deviation from its vertical path, because that is the quickest and most efficient way of getting it back to the ground. Similarly and not surprisingly, getting the bar up in the most efficient manner follows the same trajectory! Using a term from physics, whenever you deviate from the centre of gravity you create what is called a *moment arm*. The greater the moment arm, the less efficient and harder the lift will be. Hence, your aim in all of your lifts (except for the bench press and the reason for this will be explained later) should be to move the bar up and down vertically (i.e. without any forwards or backwards motion of the bar) following the centre of gravity.

This is very important! As already mentioned it will make your lifts more efficient, such that you will be able to lift heavier weights more safely. As you learn the lifts it is a very good idea to make movie recordings from the side, using a mobile phone or other device. Even when you are at a more advanced stage it is still worth doing this occasionally, because when you start lifting really heavy weights, especially for new max lifts, many people tend to focus more on the weight they are shifting than the form they are using to shift it! That is, proper form often tends to break down under heavier loads.

As has already been mentioned, people vary in terms of their body mechanics as a result of the relative proportions of their limbs and torsos. In addition, the relative position of the centre of gravity will differ between individuals dependent on the amount and distribution of body fat and/or lean muscle. Different people can also show a considerable degree of variation in joint flexibility and range of motion. For example, some have a more comfortable range of motion when the hip is rotated out to the side of the body, whereas for others this will feel very uncomfortable and their preferred and most efficient range of motion might be when the hip rotates forwards and upwards following the long axis of the body. Clearly, all these biomechanical elements will play a significant role in determining the optimum technique for squatting in any given person. This is true also for other joints and other lifts. The important point to note here is that there is no one-size-fits-all technique to any of the lifts. There are some general principles relating to core body stability for safety purposes, which need to be learned and employed during every rep. Other than that, there is a relatively large degree of freedom with regard to proper form, so long as it is reasonably comfortable for you and results in the bar following the correct trajectory with the greatest degree of efficiency.

Never underestimate the value of correct technique. The ability to perform efficiently, safely and effectively is what distinguishes elite athletes regardless of their sport. Perfecting your lifting technique at the outset is the most important part of starting in powerlifting. It is worth getting a qualified and experienced powerlifting coach (rather than a bodybuilder or regular personal trainer) to help with this initial stage of your lifting career. It is also a good idea to film your lifts from appropriate angles in order to review and appraise your progress.

The descriptions that follow contain a lot of detailed steps, all of which are important. You may find it difficult to incorporate all these instructions from the outset and if so, just add them in one or two at a time. Stick with it and in just a few weeks of training most of these individual actions will be accomplished automatically, resulting in a well executed lift. It is a bit like learning to drive – at the beginning it is difficult to do everything effectively in the right order, but after very little time you are able to execute the entire process with barely any thought.

The tripod foot

At least for the squat and deadlift, the small area represented by the soles of your feet form the only interface between your body plus its heavy load and the floor. Hence, it is extremely important that you play close attention to positioning your feet in order to maximize your stability for the duration of the lift. Your feet must form a stable base in contact with the floor and the best way to achieve this is to visualize each foot as a tripod (the base of the little toe, the base of big toe, and the heel) and to focus on displacing the pressure evenly across these three places when setting up to lift. Curling your toes slightly to 'grip' the floor can also help with stability. Once you have achieved your stable base you need to maintain it throughout the lift because any instability will likely lead to some degree of poor positioning at some point in the movement. At no point during the lift should your foot move, i.e. the foot should not rotate about the heel, the heel should not come off the ground, the toes or sides should not rock off the ground. Given the rather obvious nature of this fact, it is surprising how many non-powerlifters overlook this important element of their squat set up. Selecting the right footwear can help and this is discussed further on pages 146–147.

Breathing – the Valsalva manoeuvre

Before we get on to the lifting techniques, just a quick note on breathing as this is very important. The preferred method is to use what is called the Valsalva manoeuvre as a means for producing maximal force and stabilizing the body trunk during the lifts. The Valsalva manoeuvre involves taking in deep breaths and then holding your breath against a closed glottis. The idea is that you breath deeply into your belly, so that it expands outwards circumferentially and so allows you to brace against a lifting belt if you wear one. This generates a large increase in pressure in the cavities of the thorax and abdomen, which helps to support the spine. Your lungs should not be full to bursting as too much air makes it difficult to tense your abs properly, while too little air volume will impede your ability to brace effectively.

An additional consequence of this is a sudden rise in blood pressure and it has been suggested that this can increase the likelihood of suffering from a stroke. However, despite all the warnings you will hear, nobody has ever demonstrated a cause-and-effect relationship between strength training using the Valsalva and intracranial haemorrhage. Nonetheless, if you have a medical history of high blood pressure or other cardiovascular problems you may wish to discuss this with your GP before you start.

The problem with breathing during a set, rather than at the end once you have finished it, is that you lose most of your core body stability when you exhale completely. On the other hand, if you hold your breath for too long you might cause yourself to pass out (this can even happen on very heavy single rep sets if you get it wrong). Hence, it is best if you can hold your breath and maintain your core body rigidity throughout the set, but this may not always be possible. If you do need to breath in order to complete the prescribed number of reps in your set then you must do it at the correct point during the execution of the rep and this will be described below for each of the three lifts. Certainly, you should not be releasing your braced core when you need it the most by exhaling on the way up out of the hole during a

Breathing deeply to set the brace using the Valsalva manoeuvre immediately prior to stepping on the platform. Image credit WLM.

squat or at the top of a deadlift as many bodybuilders and personal trainers would have you believe!

Squat – the king of lifts

The squat involves supporting a bar across your upper back then lowering it by bending your knees and hips (just like sitting down on a chair), then raising it again into the upright position. This lift is often referred to as 'the king of lifts' because of the sheer amount of muscle mass activated during its execution, resulting in some serious potential for strength gains. You will see reference to both high-bar and low-bar back squats. These refer to the position of the bar on your back. As the names suggest, in the former the bar is held relatively high up on the back and in the latter it is held at the lowest possible level where rigidity can be maintained, i.e. without it slipping further down the back between reps. The low bar position is preferable because most people seem to be able to squat heavier weights using this technique. However, some people will find this position difficult to obtain at first because it requires greater shoulder mobility. If this is the case, do not worry about it, start with a high bar and try and transition to low bar later on. When transitioning from high bar to low bar (or vice versa) expect it to feel uncomfortable for a short while until you get used to it. The bar should never be positioned so high that it is resting on the back of your neck, separated from the vertebrae merely by a thin layer of skin. That is really asking for trouble!

Heavy squat training should be done in a power rack, with safety bars set at an appropriate level to support the bar if you are unable to raise it back up again (also known as getting out of the hole). The safety bars should not be set so high that they don't allow you to squat down deep enough. When using a power rack take care to remain central because if you move too much to one side as you step backwards or if you twist the position of the bar on your back, the plates on one side can hit the safety bar on the way down, which can cause an unexpected surprise and tweak your back, especially if you are coming down reasonably quickly with a heavy weight. Always make sure you set up FACING the bar as it rests in the hooks, so that you need to step out BACKWARDS once you have unracked the bar. Doing so, means that you can see what you are doing when you are re-racking the bar after a heavy squat. If you set up so that you step out forwards then you will be re-racking the bar backwards and blind and this is a recipe for disaster.

At some point you will no doubt hear or read that squatting damages your knees, and many people will tell you they don't squat for this very reason. However, this is just another of many unsubstantiated 'myths' that you will hear throughout your training. On the contrary, when done properly, squats can strengthen and tighten the connective tissue around your knees leading to increased knee stability.

The squat can be broken down as follows:

Initial set up

Position the bar in a rack so that it is level with your chest (around nipple height). With your hands twisted slightly outwards, place the fleshy part of the palm below the thumb on the bar. Duck your head under the bar and settle in so that the bar is resting on top of your rear shoulder muscles (posterior deltoids) with additional support from the upper back (trapezius) muscles. Your feet should be firmly planted on the floor, slightly more than shoulder width apart and with your toes pointed outwards slightly. As mentioned earlier, your exact foot placement will depend on

The author setting up for a low-bar squat at the All England Champion-ships, 2022. Image credit WLM.

your mobility preferences. The important point is that your midfoot is positioned directly under the bar. Your thumbs should be wrapped over the bar rather than curled underneath it. Having your thumbs in this position helps to keep the wrist aligned straight with the forearm. If you grip the bar with your thumbs wrapped under it (as you will see many people doing in the gym) then you are more likely to bend your hand too far backwards. This is highly inefficient for supporting a loaded bar because you are likely to end up supporting the weight of the bar with your wrist; it can also lead to elbow pain (tendonitis). The elbows should be held back and up as much as possible, which traps the bar into position and tightens the muscles of the upper back forming a solid platform for the bar to rest on. The ultimate aim is to get your body supporting the weight of the bar rather than your arms or wrists.

Recently, I have seen a few cases of people breaking their wrists/forearm bones whilst squatting, so it is important to make sure there is not too much strain being placed on either. One instance was a competitive lifter and it happened when they stepped forward to re-rack the bar after completing the lift. After pausing at the top of the lift, the body moved forwards rather suddenly to re-rack the bar, but the heavy bar obviously wanted to stay where it was and the sudden inertia was enough to snap the wrist. Maybe it would not have happened if the lifter had stepped forwards more slowly. In other cases, breakages have occurred due to slippage of the bar down the back after a poor set up resulting from inappropriate rack height settings. In the majority of cases, it would seem that the lifters used a very narrow grip width, which puts additional pressure on the forearm. A slightly wider grip, will still wedge the bar in place, but allows most of the weight to be supported by the upper back musculature, considerably reducing the pressure exerted on the forearms.

Getting into the correct position can be uncomfortable to begin with so do it gently and doing a few minutes of shoulder mobility warm-up exercises before you start is a very good idea. Depending on how flexible you are, you may need to move your hands slightly further out along the bar in order to get into the correct position. Take your time setting up and make sure the bar is comfortable and securely locked in before unracking it.

The author setting up to squat at the North West Masters Championships, 2022 – note the position of the thumbs over the top of the bar rather than wrapped underneath it. Image credit FMX.

The author in the start position after unracking the bar and stepping backwards at the All England Championships, 2022. Image credit WLM.

Once you have established a comfortable training set up, it is worth measuring the height of the bar from the floor using a regular tape measure and then use the same height when working out your rack height at competition (more on this later).

Unracking the bar and stepping backwards

Focus on something that will form a fixed reference point throughout your lift, whilst keeping your head in a neutral position, i.e. not bending your neck to look upwards. The reference point should be below head height, maybe even on the floor and not too far in front of you. Take a deep belly breath, hold it and brace your abdominal muscles. Then lift the bar up by straightening up your legs and lower back.

Remove the bar from the rack forcefully as this will make the weight feel lighter and give you confidence to complete the lift itself. Take two steps backwards in order to give yourself sufficient distance from the rack then hold this position with your chest raised, which tightens the lower back muscles and prevents you from leaning forwards. Your toes and knees should be pointing outwards slightly. The stepping backwards takes some practice (as does everything). If you step directly backwards you will likely end up with your feet much closer together than when you started out, purely as a result of your natural hip mechanics. In order to end up with your feet the same distance apart as when you started, swing your feet out to the side slightly as you step backwards. Try and limit the number of steps you take to just two, rather than five or six or even ten! You will see people using multiple steps, but remember that every step you take with a heavy bar on your back will sap a certain amount of energy that could be otherwise better utilized! Note: if you need to rise onto your toes in order to lift the bar out of the hooks, then the bar has been set too high and you will need to lower it.

Lowering the bar

From the erect and motionless start position, maintain your focus on your fixed reference point, take another deep breath (or two) if needed, hold it firmly and brace your core by pushing out your abdominal muscles (you will feel the pressure build up as you push these against the belt if you are wearing one). Note, you are essentially trying to force you belly outwards rather than suck it inwards and you need to maintain this rigidity throughout the entire lift, i.e. until you have raised the bar back up again. Start the downwards motion with your hips, closely followed by bending at your knees. Just imagine you are sitting down on a chair! Your knees should track outwards following the direction that your feet are pointed in and you may need to make a conscious effort to make sure this happens. Do not allow your knees to move too far forwards of your toes (they will move forwards to some degree but the more vertical you keep your lower leg the better). Your back will lean forwards into the lift as your hips bend, but keep it straight and keep your chest as high as possible in order to maintain the tightness of your lower back. If you lean too far forwards this will take the bar out of its vertical path and it will take considerable energy reserves to correct the error and stop yourself from toppling over forwards.

The important thing now is to make sure you squat down to sufficient depth, which is the point at which the top of your thigh (the thigh crease) just passes the level of

The author hitting depth at the bottom of the squat (in the hole) at the All England Championships, 2022. Image credit WLM.

the top of your knee. This is really important because it recruits the largest amount of muscle mass (the quadriceps and hamstrings engage equally) to help drive the bar back up again. If you don't squat low enough the quads will do most of the work, with little input from the hamstrings, resulting in a much lower force output. Also, if you do not squat below parallel then the lift will be classed as a fail at competition (more on this later). There is little to be gained by squatting far below parallel (the so-called 'ass to grass' technique), other than removing any degree of ambiguity for competition referees (and this is not a bad thing to do, especially on your opening lift). Once you get to the correct depth do not relax. You need to maintain your total core rigidity until you have got the bar back up to the start position (and preferably until you have re-racked it).

The author raising the bar back to the start position at the All England Championships, 2022. Image credit WLM.

Raising the bar

Also known as getting 'out of the hole,' the key here is to drive the hips up first (the so-called hip drive) and allowing the legs, back and chest to follow the natural course that this hip drive creates. Trying to force the bar upwards and backwards with your chest will reduce the impact of the hip drive. However, it is important to have the chest move upwards at the same rate as the hips. If the hips raise up but the torso does not, the bar will move outside your centre of gravity and you will fall forwards and once this starts to happen it can be very difficult to recover.

The more explosive you are out of the hole, the easier it is to get the bar back to the start position at the top of the lift. For this reason it is best to train your squats with explosivity in mind, even during your warm-up sets. For loads above 50% of your one rep max drive the bar out of the hole as explosively as you possibly can. Being too explosive below this weight risks possible injury through hyperextending your joints at lock-out.

Try not to have the bar bouncing around too much when you get it back up to the top. It may look and sound cool as the plates clang together, but it will sap your energy. Once you are back in the starting position you are ready to re-rack the bar or to perform the next rep of the set.

Re-racking the bar

Once you have got the bar back up to its starting position simply walk it forwards back into the rack until it hits the uprights then lower it back into the supporting hooks. Do this slowly in order to minimize physical stress on the wrists due to the sudden inertia of moving forwards. Lower the bar gently into the hooks and double check that it is safely in on both sides before you start to loosen your grip. At some point you will misrack the bar, so double checking you are in the correct position before you relax your hold on it will help you correct the error. If you need to rise onto your toes in order to get the bar over and into the hooks, then the rack height setting is too high.

Breathing point

Before you lower down into the squat or when the bar has come to a stop at the top of getting out of the hole. Do not exhale while you are in the hole or on the way back up (as is traditionally instructed by most personal trainers) because you will lose all your rigidity and stability when you need it the most.

Common mistakes you will see others making

Starting with the bar set too high on the rack (safety hazard when trying to return a heavily laden bar); unracking the bar facing forwards rather than backwards (safety hazard when trying to return a heavily laden bar); taking too many steps backwards following unracking the bar (wastes too much energy); not reaching a sufficient depth or locking out the knees at the top of the lift (start and finish); not collapsing the hips and knees at the same time during the initial part of the squat; leaning too far forwards on the way up out of the hole, maybe even raising the heels off the ground; knees caving inwards during the upward phase of the lift. Not keeping the feet firmly planted on the floor throughout the upward movement of the lift.

Bench Press

The bench press involves lying on a bench and lowering a barbell from an arms-locked out position until it touches the chest, then after a one-second pause, returning it to the original start position before re-racking it. This lift is the most popular lift done in any gym anywhere in the world – whenever you walk in a gym you will probably see somebody performing it, but whether or not they are doing it correctly is another matter entirely.

The bar can be held with a wide grip (hands far apart), a close grip (hands slightly more than shoulder width apart), or anywhere in between. When your hands are placed further apart the main muscular force is produced by the relatively large chest muscles. When they are placed closer together the generating force is transferred to the shoulder and triceps muscles, which are smaller. Hence, in theory, it should be possible to press heavier weights if the hands are positioned further apart and this set up also has the added advantage of the bar having to travel a shorter distance before the arms lock-out, when compared to a narrower grip. Nonetheless, it is still possible to press exceedingly heavy weights using the narrow grip position and, as with all the lifts, there is no 'one-size-fits-all' rule. If you are learning this lift for the first time then start off with a wide grip and see how you get on, though ultimately your grip width will be determined by your personal preference. You can also start of relatively narrow and gradually work your hands out slightly further apart as you progress.

Three important points to remember:

1. This is a full-body lift when done correctly and should be hard work for the entire body. If this is not the case then you are not doing it properly.

2. The height of the standard competition bench is 42–45 cm. This will not necessarily be the case for non-competition benches found in many private and commercial gyms. Any bench significantly lower or higher when you are training will obviously impact on how you set up and drive with your legs at competition. It is worth measuring your training bench to see how close it is and to try and correct any deficit that may exist, e.g. by raising it on a plank of wood etc.

3. You must respect this lift at all times because if you don't it can be dangerous (potentially fatal). Make sure you get somebody to spot for you (see below) when you try this lift for the first time or when lifting heavy. Alternatively, perform the lift in a power rack with the safety bars set at an appropriate height. There are plenty of very nasty gym fail movie clips online, most of which could have been avoided by following some very basic safety guidelines

The bench press can be broken down as follows:

Initial set-up

Take a deep breath, brace your core, then lie back on the bench with your head in a position where your eyes are directly under or just forwards of the bar. If you set up with your eyes behind the bar you are likely to catch the hooks with the bar during your reps. Take a grip of the bar making sure your hands are spread equally to ensure balance. There are rings on the bar that you can use as markers. Your wrists should be aligned straight with your forearms so that the bar is sitting on the fleshy part of the palm at the base of the thumb. This will result in the long-bones of the forearm helping to support the weight of the bar (do not let your wrist bend backwards for the same reason discussed above under the squat). Wrist wraps applied correctly over the back of the hand can prevent your wrists from bending backwards.

The thumbs must always be wrapped around the bar (rather than placed over the top as described for the squat set up). The so-called thumbless grip on the bench press (which many people actually do!) is also referred to as a suicide grip for very good reason – the last thing you want is for a heavily laden bar to slip out of your hands! Of course, this can still happen regardless of the grip used, but it is more likely with a thumbless grip. Having your thumb wrapped around the bar also allows you to grip the bar much more tightly resulting in greater activation or arm and shoulder stabilizing muscles. The harder you squeeze the greater the recruitment of muscles in the hands and forearm and the lighter the loaded bar will feel (try lifting the same weight with relaxed hands and see how much heavier it feels!).

Next, engage your upper back muscles by pulling your shoulders down and back along the bench. You need to imagine that you are trying to grip the bench with your upper back muscles, in order to provide a firm base of support from which to control and press the bar. Finally, imagine that you are trying to bend the bar slightly. This action will engage the large muscles (the lats) down the lateral margins of your chest. All of your upper body should now be tight and ready for the task.

Your feet should be firmly planted flat on the ground in a wide position with your heels under your knees. Tense your glutes and generate force through your legs by pushing down on your heels which will create a lower back arch. This will provide the so-called leg drive and will help to transfer force through your body and up to your chest to assist with the press. If your legs are too short to reach the ground comfortably you can use flat surfaced plates, or blocks not exceeding 30 cm in total height and a minimum dimension of 60 x 40 cm, to 'raise the surface of the platform'. Blocks in the range of 5 cm, 10 cm, 20 cm and 30 cm, should be made available for foot placement at all international competitions. For other competitions it is worth checking that blocks will be available, but there is no harm in bringing your own just in case. You will need to get them approved by the head referee before the competition starts.

Your lower back muscles should be tightened, which will help to create the slightly arched position, whereby it should be possible for somebody to slide their fist between your lower back and the bench, but your bottom needs to remain in contact with the bench at all times. In addition to helping to tighten your core (along with tensing your abdominal muscles) this position has the added advantage that it raises your chest slightly, hence reducing the distance the bar needs to travel during the lift. If the entire body is not tight with the core fully engaged throughout the entirety of the lift, the force from the leg drive will not be transferred through to the upper body and so will be wasted.

Everybody has their own individual way of generating their back arch and the degree of arching varies according to individual preference. Certainly at some point you will see folks climbing up on the bench like a crab in order to get into the greatest arch that they can manage. While this is OK in the gym it is no longer permissible at IPF competitions because placing the feet on the bench during set-up was banned from 2023 onwards.

Unracking the bar

Find a focal point on the ceiling directly above you and keep your eyes focused on

The author in the bench press start position with the arms locked-out at the All England Championships, 2022. Image credit WLM.

it until you have re-racked the bar at the end of the lift. Make sure your full-body is tight, with a good core brace and that you are prepared to take the weight of the bar, then have a spotter assist you in unracking the bar and getting it in balance at the start position. Lock your elbows out straight immediately (important safety issue) before moving the bar into the start position, which is held at balance directly over your chest and in line with your shoulders (i.e. the point of rotation), with your elbows still locked-out. Note, this will also be the lock-out position at the completion of the lift, so just make a mental note of where the bar is in relation to your fixed focal point on the ceiling. Your spotter (if properly trained) will check that you are ready to take the weight of the bar before releasing the full weight of it under your control. A brief nod of your head should indicate that you are ready. Do not enter into dialogue with the spotter as you will release the internal pressure you have generated to maintain your core body rigidity. Once proficient at the lift you can train without a spotter for lighter training sets.

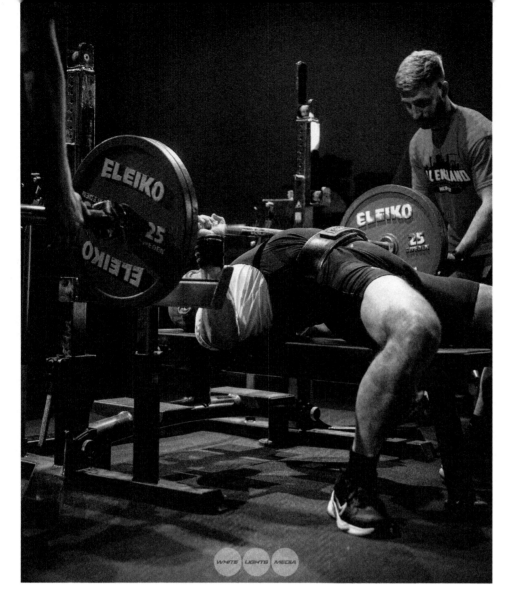

The author in the bench press paused position at the bottom of the lift at the All England Championships, 2022 – note the position of the bottom of the elbow below the top of the shoulder joint, as per the new IPF rules introduced from January 2023. Image credit WLM.

Lowering the bar

Make sure your chest is raised as much as possible, that your upper back muscles are still tight and trying to grip the bench and that your lower back is still arched (you need to make a conscious effort in order to maintain this position throughout the lift). Lower the bar gently (not too quickly) until it comes to a rest on your chest slightly forward of its starting position. Rather than just letting the bar drop downwards, imagine that you are pulling the bar down to your chest and this will help you keep tightness in your lats. It is important to maintain full-body tightness at the bottom of the lift, otherwise the weight of the bar will likely move you into a less efficient position for the all important press back up.

In effect what you are doing is bringing the bar down in a slight arc. Although this will create a short moment arm which will reduce the efficiency of the movement in terms of loading, it is necessary in order to protect the shoulder from impingement damage, which can occur if you hold the upper arms outwards at 90 degrees to

the body during this lift. If you were to bring the bar down directly, without creating a moment arm, the rotator cuff tendon could get trapped in the shoulder joint and potentially be damaged as a result of the repeated action. By reducing the angle of the upper arms this problem will be avoided, i.e. rather than have your humerus flared out at 90 degrees to the body, tuck your elbows inwards slightly so that the humerus is at approximately 45 degrees to the long axis of the body.

Throughout the entire movement your forearms should remain vertical directly under the bar. Hence, it is impossible to state a preferred touch-point on the chest because this will be determined by the degree of arch and the relative limb lengths of the lifter. Of course, the higher the touch point the better, as the bar will have less distance to travel, but do not strive for this at the expense of a manageable moment arm and also note that the bottom of the elbows need to descend below the top of the shoulder joint in order for the lift to pass at competition. If you are unable to keep your forearms vertical then try altering your grip position before you unrack the bar next time.

To make the best use of leg drive, imagine you are loading your legs on the descent, such that they are taking much of the weight, in preparation for recoil during the ascending phase of the lift.

Raising the bar

As soon as you pause with the bar lightly touching your chest remain very tight. Do not relax and allow the bar to sink into your chest because you will find it harder to get the bar moving again. Hold the bar in place for a pause of one second, then drive it back up along the same trajectory that it came down, until it ends up in balance at the same starting position in line with your shoulders and with your elbows locked-out. An advanced technique proposed by Andy Bolton for intermediate lifters is to 'pulse your bench.' This involves getting even tighter as soon as the bar touches your chest, by squeezing your glutes and fists even more, whilst driving your heels into the floor even harder.

As with the squat, you need to be as explosive as you can during the initial part of the ascent phase. A substantial speed of the bar off the chest and through to lock-out is paramount for developing a big bench press (force = mass x acceleration).

Keep your elbows tucked in and think about pushing your body away from the bar as you press it towards the ceiling. Employ leg drive to help you fire the bar upwards but make sure your bum does not rise off the bench as you do so because this will be classed as a failed lift at competition. Everyone has a slightly different

The author in the bench press pause position at the North West Masters Championships, 2022 – note the optimal touch point with vertical forearms and straight wrists, thus providing the best possible support for the heavy load. Image credit WLM.

optimal leg and foot position to prevent the bum rising, so you will need to experiment to find what works best for you. If you find your bum rising try moving your feet further backwards and/or further out sideways from the bench. Pushing down though your heels can cause your bum to rise up, so try to generate leg drive force by driving your feet forwards instead (imagine you are trying to push your toes through the front of your shoe). Getting this right takes time and practice but is well worth it because it will increase your bench.

Some lifters prefer to raise the bar using the 'j-curve' method, whereby instead of following the same trajectory back up, they bring the bar towards their shoulders first and then press it back up, though still returning it to the same locked-out starting point. What this does is reduces the moment arm more quickly, which in theory should allow the lifter to shift a heavier load. However, this technique takes the bar closer to your neck and face (so if you have an accident it could be a nasty one) and it requires a slightly longer bar path.

Re-racking the bar

Once your elbows are locked-out you will be able to allow the bar to fall back safely towards the rack uprights and then lower it into the hooks. Do not attempt to move the bar towards the rack before your elbows are locked-out because this will create a very hazardous situation, whereby if you lose control of the weight it can fall on your neck or face! This will not happen if the elbows are locked-out over your chest and shoulders beforehand. For the same reason, do not start to lower the bar into the hooks until you feel it make contact with the uprights. If you have a spotter they will help you direct the bar back to the rack, but you need to maintain control of the weight until it is safely back in its hooks.

Breathing point

If you need to breathe between reps then this should be done once the bar has come to a stop at the top of the press and is balanced over the shoulders.

Common mistakes you will see others making

Not lowering the bar far enough that it touches the chest, or if it does then not pausing the bar on the chest for long enough (touch and go); not having the feet set firmly on the floor which translates to not having a sufficient leg drive to facilitate the lift (you will often see people bench pressing on their toes, or even worse, with their feet dancing around all over the place); not locking the elbows out fully before starting the lift or when re-racking the bar (this is a serious safety issue); lifting with a thumbless grip and/or arms flared out at 90 degrees to the body. There are plenty of other mistakes that are commonly made though these can be more difficult to spot, such as not having a sufficient arch in the lower back and not setting and maintain the upper back support throughout tho lift.

Using a spotter

The role of a spotter is to help you unrack the bar (should you wish them to do so) and to help you re-rack it in the event that you get into any difficulty with the weight. You will no doubt see people helping others this way in any gym that you walk into. Indeed, it is imperative that you use a spotter if you are not confident with the weight you are aiming to bench, because if you get into trouble without a spotter serious injury or even death (very rarely) may be the end result! Alternatively, if no spotter is available you can conduct the bench press inside a power rack with safety bars set at an appropriate height to save you if you get into trouble.

As with many other things, not all spotters are created equal! For your own safety it is important that your spotter is competent. You need to agree in advance what it is you are hoping to achieve with the set. Importantly, if the spotter is helping you to unrack the bar then you need to clarify how your spotter will know when it is OK for them to release the bar under your full control. Similarly, you need to clarify what cue your spotter should use as a signal from you that you need help raising the bar. The last thing you want is for your spotter to be too eager to get involved with what is essentially your lift! If they touch the bar or assist in any other way before you have managed to lock it back out at the top then that particular rep does not count!

Some common ways that spotters can interfere with the effectiveness of your bench press include touching the bar with their fingers (or even grabbing hold of it) as you are raising it, touching your elbows to help push up your bar, leaning over your face and shouting encouragement at you, resulting in the double whammy of blocking your line of sight to your focal point (made even worse if they are wearing a baseball cap – ask them to turn it around before you start) and spitting/dribbling on you. Some spotters will also try and push you to do more reps than you actually set out to do, thinking that they are doing you a favour by getting as much out of you as possible (remember, it's your program, don't let others take charge of it!). More serious problems include releasing the bar before you are fully prepared to take the weight of it and not making sure that the bar is re-racked properly before turning around and walking away! Both of these can lead to some seriously unpleasant consequences!

If you do get into trouble do not expect your spotter to take the full weight of the bar! The spotter is there to help you get the bar re-racked safely, so you still need to use as much power as you have available to assist with the process. If you give up completely and expect the spotter to take all the weight you will end up with a very nasty surprise and most likely a serious injury! If you see your spotter messing around with their mobile phone or otherwise distracted while you are doing the set, re-rack the bar and find another spotter. As a rule of thumb, if a person does not bench heavy then they are unlikely to be a competent spotter. Conversely, just because somebody does bench heavy does not necessarily mean they will be a great spotter.

Deadlift – the queen of lifts

The deadlift involves pulling a bar up off the floor until the legs and torso lock-out straight, pausing for a second, then lowering it back down again to the start position. This lift should be where you are able to generate the most power. There are two different techniques: sumo – where the legs are spread wide apart and the bar is gripped and raised with the arms between the legs, and conventional – where the legs are placed closer together and the bar is gripped and raised with the arms held to the outside of the legs. Semi-sumo is a version of sumo, where the feet are not placed so wide apart, but the arms are still between the legs when gripping the bar.

Conventional wisdom has it that the sumo lift presents a shorter distance that the bar has to move in order to complete the lift, making it a little easier to complete; conversely it is often said that heavier weights can ultimately be lifted using the conventional style. One advantage of sumo is that it allows the lifter to maintain a more vertical torso throughout the lift, so might be preferred by people with a history of lower back injury who may be worried about lifting heavy loads conventionally. If you are just starting out try both and if you have no preferred style then opt for conventional.

Options for gripping the bar

You will see people using two different grip types. The standard technique is to have both hands oriented in the same direction, i.e. with palms facing towards you (the double overhand grip). This produces rotational symmetry of the shoulders and is the best approach because the musculature on both sides of the upper body is operating in the same manner. However, some people find it difficult to lift very heavy weights like this, so they alternate their hands as the weights get heavier such that on one side the palm is facing forwards (supinated). This puts the rotation of the shoulders out of symmetry, resulting in the musculature on the two sides working differently and opens up the risk of biceps tears in the arm with the supinated grip. To help avoid this, keep your elbows straight, tense your triceps and think 'long arms.' Given the uneven nature of lifting in this manner, it is also easier to twist and injure the hips and lower back using this technique. However, the alternate grip helps to keep the bar from swinging forwards away from your body and also prevents it from rolling out of your hands.

The author in the conventional deadlift set-up position at the North West Masters Championships, 2022 – note the straight back, raised hips and the alternate hand grip. Image credit FMX.

An alternative approach is to use the hook-grip technique with the double overhand grip. This involves wrapping your four fingers over the top of the barbell as for the standard double overhand grip, but you then trap your thumb under your index and middle fingers so that your thumb wraps around below the bar and under your fingers. Make sure you are not squeezing over the thumb knuckle. If you find it difficult or painful make sure you place the barbell back on the floor before releasing your grip. The hook grip offers a symmetrical and more secure pulling option for heavy singles or competition lifts, making drops and injuries much less likely, although people with small hands or short digits will struggle with this technique. It can be awkward and sometimes painful at first, but can offer significant benefits once you get used to it. You can use medical tape on your thumbs to reduce discomfort when you first try this technique, but remember that no gains are worth serious injury. According to the IPF rulebook two layers of medical tape are allowed in competition.

You will often see people using lifting straps when performing deadlifts. However, straps are not permitted in powerlifting competition so there is no point in using them during your regular deadlift training. All you will do is compromise your grip strength development which in turn will impact on how much you can pull off the floor at competition.

Unless you are training in a dedicated powerlifting facility you are unlikely to have access to competition specification plates, the largest of which have a diameter of 45 cm. Your training plates will likely be somewhat smaller than this which means the bar will sit lower down relative to the same weight at competition. Essentially, you will be permanently training deficit deadlifts unless you make a correction to raise the bar slightly. Training a slight deficit is not necessarily a bad thing as it should make moving the same load feel slightly easier on competition day (though see comment about bumper plates on pages 184–185).

The deadlift is relatively simple and can be broken down as follows:

Initial set-up

Stand in front of the bar with your feet slightly narrower than shoulder width apart (or wider if using the sumo technique), toes pointing forwards or slightly outwards and with your shins approximately two centimetres away from the bar, such that the bar is positioned above your shoe lace ties. The bar will be resting directly over the middle of the foot, resulting in the optimal trajectory of the bar during the lift (most people do not set up close enough to the bar!). From this point on the bar must not move until you lift it off the ground, because you already have it in the correct position. Take a deep breath, hold it and force your abdominal muscles out against your belt (if you are wearing one), grip the floor with your toes then bend at the waist keeping your legs and back straight and grip the bar just to the outside of your legs (don't move the bar!). Now move your shins forwards until they touch the bar and direct your knees out very slightly towards your arms, but do not push the bar forwards.

Raise your chest without dropping your hips (in the ideal position your back will be straight and your shoulders will be positioned very slightly over and in front of the bar; your hips will be considerably higher than your knees – this is not a squat!). This will create tightness in your lower back. Your arms should be as close to vertical as possible regardless of whether you are pulling sumo or conventional. Finally, engage your lats and take the slack out of the bar with a quick jerk of your arms, then build up tension by initiating the pull but not with enough force to lift the bar off the ground. Your entire body should feel nice and tight.

Your descent to the bar should be slow and controlled, maintaining tightness and focus all the way. The idea being the harder it is to get down, the easier it is to get back up. Increased tension generates more strength and lowers the potential for injury.

Lifting the bar

Pull the bar upwards keeping it in contact with your legs the entire time and lock-out straight with the bar at around hip height, by pushing your hips forwards and raising your chest. Do not over extend this forward hip movement. You will see people who do this and end up leaning too far backwards. The longer you spend in the set up position the more it will sap your energy. Hence, the best approach, once you have become proficient in the set-up, is to rip the bar off the floor as quickly as possible (grip it and rip it!). Essentially, the first part of the lift is like a standing leg-press, so try using the mental cue 'leg-press the floor', as this will help you to recruit the larger muscles of the legs and hips. You will feel like you are pressing the bar off the floor with the large muscles of your legs rather than pulling it off the floor with the smaller muscles of your lower back. The faster you manage to pull the bar off the floor the greater is the likelihood of getting it to lock-out as opposed to hitting

The author in
the conventional
deadlift set-
up position
at the North
West Masters
Championships,
2022.

Opposite page:
The author in
the semi-sumo
deadlift set-up
position at his
first Novice
competition,
2018. Image
credit LD.

The author in
the conventional
deadlift lock-
out position
at the North
West Masters
Championships,
2022.

Opposite page:
The author in
the semi-sumo
deadlift lock-
out position at
his first Novice
competition,
2018. Image
credit LD.

a sticking point on the way up. Once you get the bar past your knees drive your hips forwards to complete the lift. Everything needs to move at the same pace. Your bum must never move up quicker than your shoulders because doing so will create excessive strain on your lower back.

Lowering the bar

After you have held the raised bar in position for a second or so, unlock the hips first and slide the bar back down the legs until it passes the knees, at which point the knees bend to finish the movement. Do not drop the bar! The descent must be controlled for its full length and the bar should finish at the same position from which it started. Be careful not to smash the bar into the top of your knees on the way back down (this can happen if you break at the knees first rather than the hips). Also keep an eye on your toes if using an extremely wide-stanced sumo technique. The rep is not complete until the bar is back on the ground and it is important to maintain your core rigidity and straight back as much as possible until this time. You will often see lifters who neglect to do this and start rounding their back well before the bar is back on the floor.

Breathing point

Between reps when the bar is on the floor. Do not exhale at the top of the lift because you will significantly weaken the core body support that is being used to hold the bar in place.

Common mistakes you will see others making

Starting with the bar positioned too far away; lifting with a rounded back; setting up with the hips too low (in too much of a squat-like position); lifting and lowering the bar so it follows a trajectory too far in front of the body; not controlling the bar properly on the way down; not locking out fully at the top of the lift (or over-exaggerating the lock-out); releasing core body rigidity before the bar is back on the floor (though this can sometimes be difficult to observe); not allowing the bar to come to a full stop before starting the next rep (in this case the lifter is relying on the touch and go method in the hope that a slight bounce in the bar will facilitate the upward lift of the next rep. Given that the main work, and hence benefit, of this lift comes from raising a static bar off the ground, it needs to be done from a dead stop position).

Set up rituals

In the preceding explanations of how to conduct the lifts correctly I have explained how best to set up with the bar before unracking it and these approaches are just fine for a new lifter. However, what you will notice relatively quickly is that other people often perform various different 'rituals' as they approach the bar and set up for the lift. You may see this in gyms, but you will certainly see it on the competition platform. Such rituals may include pacing up and down, listening to certain music, verbalizations, limb movements aimed at engaging certain muscles, using smelling salts, applying chalk, wraps, etc. in a certain way, screwing or drilling their feet into the floor etc. or various combinations thereof. The list is endless and each lifter has their own idiosyncrasies and it won't be too long until you do too. Such rituals are developed gradually over time and build on success. If doing something a certain way leads to a successful result then the same thing is repeated the next time in order to achieve success once again. Consequently, such rituals may have a real effect or just a perceived effect. So long as they help you get in the groove for your lift (and are not so extreme that they disturb other people) it doesn't really matter. Although everybody will have slightly (or significantly) different rituals, most will be based on common themes that have proven beneficial to lifters in the past. For this reason it is worth observing some of the more common types of pre-lift practices because you may be able to incorporate some of them to produce success in your own lifting.

Form creep

The aim of any powerlifter is perfect execution of the lift within the very narrow parameters of biomechanical efficiency as determined by his or her anthropometry, but form creep (a term coined by Mark Rippetoe in his *Starting Stength* book) during training will manifest itself unless you make a determined effort to prevent it. Form creep occurs when the ability to perform a movement pattern with precision degrades gradually over time. The initial minor variance and subsequent slight changes may go unnoticed by the lifter, but can accumulate over time to a point where the lift is no longer being performed to competition standard (e.g. not hitting depth in the squat). Even at this point, if the multiplication of the error has been slow enough over time then the lifter will still be unaware of this form creep and is liable to get a nasty shock the next time they step on the competition platform. Examples of form creep errors to watch out for include: depth, back angles and hip rotation in the squat; grip width, back arch, leg drive and elbow position in the bench press; stance width, distance from the bar and hip height in the deadlift.

Any good coach will pick up on form creep before it becomes an issue, but those who train alone will need to record and critically appraise their technique as often as possible. Make sure you record from different angles as constantly recording from the side (e.g. for squat depth) will miss stance set-up asymmetries, which can also be a problem. There are numerous mobile phone apps that will track your bar path and speed and these can be very useful for assessing form and consistency.

Accessory lifts

In addition to training the main competition lifts you will need to train a range of different accessory lifts, the aim of which is to increase core body strength and to strengthen the associated musculature that supports the large muscle groups involved in the main lifts. Accessory work can also help to avoid muscle imbalances that can result from training only the main lifts. For example, those who bench press a lot but do very little to strengthen their rear delts can end up with their shoulders pulled forwards, leading to impingement issues. Variations of the main lifts are particularly useful as accessories.

Additional resistance aids such as thick rubber bands and heavy chains can be utilized in various different ways for each of the three main lifts. When anchored below the bar, resistance bands increase the intensity of the lift towards lock-out and so are useful to help prevent sticking points towards the top of the lift. Chains work in a similar way. The intensity of the lift increases as more links come off the ground as the bar is raised and conversely, the bar is essentially unloaded as it lowers and the chain links accumulate on the ground.

Another option concerns weight releasers (also known as eccentric hooks), which are large metal hooks that can be loaded with plates to help you overload the eccentric or lowering phase of the bench press or squat. They hook over the barbell and safely detach from it when they touch the ground allowing greater explosiveness through the concentric movement as the lighter load is pushed up back to the start position. This accentuated eccentric training increases both your eccentric and concentric strength. They are also one of the best tools for overcoming fear of very heavy weights and will increase your confidence with near-maximal weights prior to new 1RM attempts.

Some examples of accessory lifts are provided below, but there are many others. The exercises selected will of course depend upon the equipment you have available. Some of the following exercises are useful for more than one lift, for example, the Jefferson squat/deadlifts, leg press and various back hyperextension work, good mornings etc. involve movement patterns that will help with both squat and deadlift. Exercises that work the upper back muscles, e.g. face-pulls, T-bar rows, pull ups (and chin ups) etc. will also have carry over between the lifts. Grip strength training is useful to help avoid dropping heavy deadlifts.

Many of the accessory lifts listed below may at first appear to be rather simple in terms of their execution, although as with many things, this is rarely the case. Each lift has its own nuances and so it is important to make sure you understand how to conduct the lift or use the equipment correctly and safely before you start. A quick search online will provide plenty of information on the correct form for any of the lifts listed below. Alternatively, a staff member in the gym where you train should be able to advise you in terms of how to use the equipment available.

Squat accessories

Paused squats: As for normal squats but pause 'in the hole' at the bottom. Allows you to feel comfortable in the hole and teaches your core how to stay stiff under the bar. It allows you to feel all the muscles that you should be using to brace properly with a heavier squat.

Box squats: Similar to the above but you squat down to sit and pause on a box. This can be placed on a pile of rubber mats so the height can be reduced gradually by removing one mat at a time. It has flexibility benefits for new lifters unable to hit depth and for more experienced lifters who cannot break parallel with their light warm-up weights, or for those who tend to cut depth as they approach their maximum. Lifters will always break parallel, or any other desired depth when they have to sit on a box at the bottom of the lift. Do not bounce off the box as this is inviting injury. Rather, pause on the box before returning back to the upright position. This will develop explosive power at the bottom of the lift to get you out of the hole.

Tempo squats: As for normal squats but done slowly. Has the benefit of allowing you to focus on the movement and on hitting depth, whilst also increasing time-under-tension.

Jefferson squats: Not quite a squat and not quite a deadlift, but still a full-body compound lift and great for developing core strength, with much reduced stress on the lower back compared to a regular deadlift. In this lift you set up by standing over the bar with one leg either side of it in a shoulder-width stance. Hinge from your hips and bend your knees to lower yourself to the bar, with your front hand suppinated and your rear hand pronated. Grasp the bar with straight arms, tense your core (to stop your body rotating as you lift) and push against your firmly planted feet to raise the bar off the ground until your legs lock-out at the top, then return the bar to the ground. This lift takes some getting used to but it is well worth the effort. Make sure you remember to swap foot and hand positions between sets in order to work both sides of the body equally.

Safety bar squats: These are a good option for new lifters or for experienced lifters who just fancy a bit of a change in their routine. The industrial padding makes for considerably greater comfort when compared to a bare barbell supported across the back and shoulders. They are also a good for working around certain minor injuries or for those dealing with shoulder mobility/ impingement issues. Bow (or Duffalo) bars are also similar in this last respect.

Front squats: Great for developing the quads, glutes, upper back, core and even biceps. You can either start with the bar in a rack or clean if off the floor for a bit of explosivity training.

Zercher squats: Zerchers have the bar held in the crook of the elbows and strengthens the upper back, arms and legs. Elbow sleeves and a foam barbell pad will help to minimise discomfort with heavy loads.

Zombie (also known as Frankenstein) squats: The bar rests on the anterior delts with the arms stretched out forwards ... like a zombie! In this variation, the bar is not held in the hands and so you really need to focus on maintaining correct technique, with the body upright in order to prevent the bar rolling forwards along your arms.

Banded/chained squats: The use of bands and chains was briefly mentioned earlier, but they are included again here as these variable-load lifts are particularly effective as squat accessories. The weight decreases as you lower the bar and the chain links gather on the ground, such that the lift is lightest out of the hole at the bottom and gets progressively heavier as you return to lock-out. Supporting the bar with bands from above (in a power rack) takes off some of the load at the bottom of the lift, which will allow you to train the lock-out range of the lift with heavier loads.

Machine squats: These come in various guises, including hack squat, linear hack squat, pendulum squat, belted squat, etc. If you don't have access to a belted squat machine you can fashion a workable alternative using a dipping belt, loading pin and wooden boxes. A decent leg press machine is also useful for overload training.

Lunges, Bulgarian split squats, Sissy squats: Gym staples that can be done with either bodyweight or dumbbells, kettlebells, etc.

Heavy walk outs: Set up in the rack with a weight above your current squat PB, building up gradually to 110–115%. Unrack the bar and step out to the squat start position and hold for 15 seconds before re-racking the bar. Make sure you set the safety bars appropriately!

High pin squats: Another overload option for weights that are too heavy to squat through the full range of motion. Set the rack pins high up so that you can move the weight through this limited range of motion. Gradually lower the pins as you make progress and begin to feel more confident with the heavy weight.

Various leg/isolation machines: Examples commonly found in many gyms include: leg extension (quads), hamstring curls (lying, standing or seated), leg press, hack squat, calf raises, etc.

Bench press accessories

Overhead press (also known as shoulder press, military press, strict press or standing press): This is a great lift for general upper body strength and should really be trained as a main compound lift rather than an accessory, but it is listed here as such because it is not an official powerlifting competition lift. In short, the lift involves pressing a barbell from your chest to lock-out directly over your head, then returning it back to the start position. You can either start with it set in a rack or clean it off the floor for more of an explosive impact.

Inclined bench press: Pressing on an inclined angle shifts the tension to your upper chest and requires more effort from your shoulders. It is a good option for overall upper body muscle development rather than for addressing particular weak points.

Declined bench press: In this variation the bench is set in a declined position. Many will argue that there is little to be gained from this lift in terms of developing greater strength. However, benefits include additional lower chest muscle growth, which can enhance general pressing strength. It also decreases potential strain on the shoulders that can result from regular flat and incline benching.

Narrow grip bench press: Similar to a regular bench, but with the hands placed approximately shoulder width apart, or narrower if comfortable. This lift focuses the effort on the triceps.

Bow (Duffalo) bar bench press: This specialist bar has a curved middle region between the sleeves and is beneficial as a bench press accessory because it increases the range of motion at the bottom of the lift. The bend in the bar forces the lifter to bring their arms down further in order to touch the bar to the chest, when compared to a regular barbell. This results in more effort from the chest musculature to press the barbell back up, so is useful when the weak point is getting the bar off the chest. Lifters with shoulder problems should be cautious about using this bar because it could challenge the range of motion at the shoulders too much, especially when loaded with plates. By contrast, this bar can reduce strain on the shoulders when used for squatting.

Spoto press: Consider it as a paused bench press, but with the pause being at a point slightly off your chest rather than on it. This reduces the stretch at the bottom of the lift and forces you to maintain greater tension whilst working through your weak-point portion of the lift. The position at which you pause will depend on where in the normal bench press range of motion you start to slow down and feel weak. It is a good idea to record your lift in order to determine where this point is, as what you perceive to be the case may be different from the reality.

Heavy holds: Set up on the bench and work up to a weight approximately 125% of your current PB (work up gradually and go heavier if you feel comfortable doing so). Have a spotter hand out the bar to you. Keep your elbows locked but let the weight settle into your shoulders and chest and hold for 15 seconds before re-racking the bar. Make sure you have appropriately positioned safety bars!

Sling shot bench press: The slingshot is an elasticated upper body device for overloading the bench press. It wraps around your elbows and as you bring the barbell down during the bench press, the sling shot creates elastic tension on your chest, which allows you to move approximately 10–15% more weight than you normally would for the same number of reps. The lift operates through the full range of motion, unlike most other overloading methods which reduce the ROM. The elastic (fabric or rubber) item is sometimes marketed under different names, such as bench blaster (generic), magnum ram (Titan), etc. Alternatively you can take a heavy resistance band, double it over, then twist it once to form an 'X' in the middle and put it on your arms just like a sling shot. The magnum ram is marketed as having a multi-directional elastic core that more accurately conforms to the body's natural movement pattern and is consequently more efficient at relieving stress on the shoulder girdle, compared to other similar devices. However, the different design affects the 'groove' of the lift and some reviews suggest the sling shot is a better mimic of a raw bench press.

Board presses: The wooden boards range in thickness from one to three boards and usually have a handle that an assistant uses to position the board on your chest while you complete your bench press rep. Essentially, they decrease the range of motion of the lift, taking out the most difficult bit at the bottom and allow you to focus on increasing power through the mid-part of the press. The reduced ROM makes it possible to overload the weights in order to strengthen lock-out muscles. Start with the three-board (easiest) and work down through two to one. As an alternative, foam boards or blocks can be used that have been designed specifically for this purpose and without the need for an assistant; some are strapped around your torso, whereas others can be attached to the bar; some can be used in both ways.

Pin presses (or dead bench): Set the safety pins below your current sticking point and rest the bar across them. You then press the bar from this dead stop, thus removing all the tension that is normally built up as the bar descends in the regular movement. This will help you power through your sticking points.

Banded/chained presses: The use of bands and chains was mentioned earlier, but they are included again here as these variable-load lifts are particularly effective as bench accessories. The weight is lightest off your chest at the bottom of the lift and gets progressively heavier as you reach lock-out. Hence, it helps you emphasize explosive speed through your sticking points and trains the lock-out, but is not particularly effective for sticking points at the bottom of the lift. Supporting the bar with bands from above (in a power rack) takes off some of the load at the bottom of the lift, which will allow you to train the lock-out range of the lift with heavier loads.

Earthquake (or bamboo) bar bench presses: This highly flexible bar is designed to be used for high reps with light weights hanging off rubber bands. The swinging weights and flexible bar create a chaotic load which engages all the smaller stabilizing muscles of the shoulder girdle. The main purpose is preventative injury training or prehab to avoid problems such as impingements and rotator cuff tears. These specialist bars are expensive and rarely found in gyms.

Various dumbbell presses: Most of what can be done with a barbell can also be done with dumbbells. They have the added benefit of allowing a full range of motion, which may be impossible with a barbell, and they also work your stabilizer muscles differently. One main benefit of dumbbells is you will be able to isolate and identify unilateral deficiencies within the chest and shoulder. These imbalances are often masked when using the barbell because your stronger side overcompensates to make up for the weaker side. You see it frequently with lifters who push one side of the bar up faster than the other as they start to fatigue. Dumbbells also allow for a more natural grip, giving the wrists and elbows a little more flexibility of movement than is possible with a barbell. Use power hooks supported over a barbell for heavy dumbbell pressing work to avoid injury through lifting and swinging heavy dumbbells off the floor and into position.

Dips: Make sure your shoulders are well and truly warmed up before you begin. Start with bodyweight dips and then progress to weighted dips using a dipping belt. The difficulty of this exercise can be increased significantly by using gymnastic rings which requires much more input from stabilizing muscles. If you are unable to do a bodyweight dip some gyms have assisted dipping machines to help get you started.

Deadlift accessories

Deficit deadlifts: Same as regular deadlifts, but with a platform under your feet, requiring you to stoop lower to grab the bar. You can stand on a wooden block or just on a weight plate if pulling conventional. If pulling sumo, set up in a power rack so you can wedge the plates or boards against the inside of the rack to stop them from slipping outwards when you stand on them. Alternatively, you can just use plates of smaller diameter than competition specification plates, as this essentially lowers the bar, creating the same effect. Deficit deadlifts make the muscles responsible for strength at the bottom-end of the lift contract harder to overcome the load, which should translate into increased strength when attempting to pull maximal weights off the floor.

Paused deadlifts: Pause the lift for a moment just below the knees, then complete the lift. It essentially breaks the lift down into its two component parts – the initial push with the quads, followed by the pull resulting from driving the hips forwards. It allows you to work these two individual elements separately before combining them into a single seamless motion. It also increases time under tension and so can build muscle strength. Also, by altering the position of the pause (e.g. bottom-, mid-, top-end) the lifter can focus their attention on a particular part of the range of movement to practice their technique and address weak spot issues.

Jefferson squats/deadlifts: See this entry under squats.

Romanian deadlifts (RDLs): This lift starts from a standing position, as you would be with the deadlift at lock-out. You push your hips backwards and lower the weight to slightly below the kneecap, before returning back to the start position. The focus is on the glutes and hamstrings and it is great for posterior chain strength. RDLs use the principle of time-under-tension, with each set being performed without resetting between reps and without the plates touching the floor.

Good mornings: Essentially the same as RDLs but with the bar positioned high on the back rather than being held in the hands.

Back hyperextensions: In this exercise you lie on an inclined hyperextension bench then bend forward at the waist. Start with your bodyweight then use incremental weight increases using dumbbells, weight plates or resistance bands. It strengthens the posterior chain, especially the spinal erectors, hamstrings and glutes. I also use this to warm-up before squat and deadlift sessions. Keep your back straight and avoid hyperextending it as you return your torso back up to the start position.

Reverse hyperextensions: Similar to the above, but it is the lower body that moves rather than the upper body. The best way to do these is using a machine specifically designed for the purpose by Louie Simmons at Westside Barbell, although you will not find it in many gyms. With a little creativity it is easy enough to fashion an alternative option using resistance bands and a high table or similar. There are some DIY options for home gym set ups online.

Trap-bar (also known as Hex- or Diamond-bar) deadlifts: This is a quadriceps dominant lift with a more upright torso and is good for lifters who struggle with getting into the proper position in the barbell deadlift. Consequently, it generates less lower back (lumbar) stress, so can be useful for those who are prone to lumbar pain or who are recovering from injury. I enjoy doing this overload deadlift variation because I can lift considerably more weight with it than I can with a regular barbell. I then convince myself that if I can increase my intensity with this lift then I should be able to do so with my regular lift as well. It is a good way to keep heavy loads moving without putting too much stress on the lower back.

Block/rack pulls: Two similar overload variations, which basically involve raising the bar off the ground before starting the lift. Block pulls are pulled off wooden blocks (and have similar bar slack dynamics to a regular deadlift as the point of contact with the floor is still the weight plates) and rack pulls have the bar positioned across safety bars in a power rack. Here there is no slack in the bar as you lift it. Rack pulls tend to be somewhat easier and more so the higher the start position. These lifts prioritize load over range of motion and will give you an idea of what it feels like to lock-out a big new PB.

Isometric accessory techniques

An isometric contraction is where the muscle length does not change under load and can be achieved by pushing or pulling the barbell against rack pins, so that movement of the bar beyond the pins is impossible even if it has no weights loaded on it. The aim is to push or pull the bar as hard as possible and hold this for approximately 10 to 30 seconds, with the goal of applying maximum isometric contraction at the weak point within the range of motion.

Isometric training is generally considered an advanced training technique and can be applied to all three lifts. It is more taxing than you might imagine, so make sure you allow time for recovery from this type of training. Three important points to note are as follows:

1. Isometric techniques are only effective across a narrow range, so set the pins as close to any sticking point as possible. If your sticking point is towards the lock-out at the top of the lift, then there will be no benefit to using isometric techniques at the bottom of the lift and vice versa.

2. Isometric training loses its benefit if performed using poor positional awareness, so make sure you are replicating the weak-point position that you would be in when performing a perfectly executed lift. Maintaining the correct position throughout the remainder of the lift is also important.

3. Isometric lifts need to be executed with maximum effort in order to be effective. Just passively pushing or pulling the bar against the pin will reduce the benefit significantly.

Additional benefits of isometric training result from the dramatically increased time under tension, which helps to build larger muscle mass. It also facilitates improved motor unit recruitment, which could in turn increase overall strength and power production. The static element of the lift also allows for greater focus on the mind-muscle connection. You should be able to generate a better feeling for which muscles are being engaged and to what degree, which in turn will help identify and resolve any imbalances.

Given that the primary focus of powerlifters is to move their barbell, not halt it, it may seem counter-intuitive to purposely use isometrics as a training method. However, every lift has a sticking point when the weights get heavy enough and if you wish to try something besides dropping weight and increasing volume for a bit then it is worth considering adding isometrics to your training schedule.

Isometric core training is also suggested as part of your competition warm-up prior to squats and deadlifts because they help to generate and maintain core rigidity while causing less muscle damage and fatigue than exercise options with more dynamic eccentric actions.

Your choice of accessory lifts is best aimed at targeting current weak points in your heavy lifts. To utilize the accessories to your full advantage, you need to identify which movements will specifically cater to your current weakness. Some accessories are universally useful and will pay big dividends throughout the full range of a lift, but others are more niche and of greater benefit when tailored to a specific part of the lift.

A powerlifter who focuses on getting stronger in their accessory lifts will have a greater chance of getting stronger on the three competitive lifts as well. Hence, accessory work should not be trained with any less gusto, effort or intensity than that applied to training the main compound lifts! Train your main compound lift first, then select two or at most three accessory lifts to follow. If you feel you can easily train more than three accessory exercises then you are probably not training your main lift hard enough. Sometimes you might just fancy a couple of hypertrophy accessories to finish off a training session and get a bit of a pump and that is absolutely fine.

A simple way to help you organize your accessory lifting is to consider your work-load in a hierarchical context. For example:

Level 1: Main compound lift (i.e. squat, bench press or deadlift).
Level 2: Accessory lift that helps to address a perceived weakness at Level 1, such as a sticking point or a breakdown in form (e.g. deficit deadlift to address pulling heavier weights off the floor more easily).
Level 3: Accessory lift that helps to support the work being done in Level 2 rather than directly addressing a weak-point of Level 1 (e.g. weighted back hyperextensions in the above scenario).

There are a great many potential accessory lifts that can be used as a training aid for powerlifting and only some of the more commonly used and effective techniques have been listed here. Ultimately, the best accessory exercise will be the one that targets your weak spot whilst also reinforcing proper technique within certain ranges of motion. As with the main compound lifts, a focus on correct technique will pay dividends in the long run. Ego lifting as much weight as possible will lead to form breakdown and increase potential for injury.

Training the core

Many powerlifters have excellent looking physiques with large and popping six (or even eight) packs without actually doing any significant specific abs or core training. This physique results from performing heavy squats and deadlifts whilst bracing the abs firmly against a tightly fitted belt and eating appropriately to maintain a relatively low body fat content. However, appearance can be deceiving and whilst this may look like a super strong core the underlying reality can be rather different.

I prefer to combine the majority of my core training with my light cardio day, but also employ some isometric core training in my warm-up prior to squats and deadlifts in order to prime my core ready for these heavy lifts. I employ a broad range of abs training options (declined sit up twists, hanging crunches, captains chair knee and leg raises, kneeling rope pulley crunches, barbell/abs wheel roll outs, planks, farmers walks, etc.) in order to focus on the full range of abs, including flexion and rotation movements. However, it is also important to focus on stabilization (anti-extension, anti-rotation and anti-lateral flexion), which is the main purpose of core training for powerlifters. Single-sided farmers walks are a great way of adding an increased degree of stabilization stress.

A similar result can be achieved using kettlebell walks, again done unilaterally for the same reason. You can add a dynamic element to kettlebell walks by suspending them from a thick resistance band, so they create a degree of chaotic movement when walking to further stimulate your stabilizing muscles. Alternatively, use two different weighted kettlebells, with one carried by your side and the other held above your head. Single handed kettlebell front squats are also very good for core bracing with specific carry over to the competition squat. For additional core training you can employ regular and side planks, loaded back hyperextensions, reverse hyperextensions, tractor tyre flips, slam balls, push and pull a prowler or sled, etc.

Cardio

Cardio is often considered a four-letter-word amongst powerlifters, but your cardiovascular fitness is not something that should be neglected. Programming in one or two light cardio days each week is a good way of breaking up your lifting routine and giving your body time to recover from the heavy weights. Competitive powerlifting can be tough on your joints so it is best to avoid high impact cardio such as running, and this is especially true for heavier people. A brisk walk on an inclined treadmill can get the heart pumping and build up a sweat. You can still employ the concept of progressive overload by gradually increasing the incline, speed and/or duration of the walk. Once you have maxed out on these you can increase the training stress further by wearing a weighted vest, which you can also gradually increase the weight of. Start nice and easy and gradually work up to 60 minutes. This will help avoid the painful condition of shin splints.

If your gym is well equipped in the cardio department feel free to use a range of different machines to prevent boredom. Many gyms have a range of different cardio equipment, such as treadmills, exercise/spin/air bikes, rowers, stair climbers, Jacob's ladder, cross-trainers, ski (SkiErg) machines, etc. Remember though, you are a powerlifter and this is supposed to be a (active) rest day, so keep it relatively light. Also, choose to walk more in your daily routines rather than taking the car. For example, ditching the car for the school run, which has the added benefit of also being beneficial for your kids.

Training for power over strength

All the aforementioned elements of training have focused on strength training as opposed to training for power. Although the two are closely related, there is a distinct difference in that power specifically refers to generating force in a given unit of time. To explain this more simply, strength refers to how much you can lift, but power relates to how quickly you can lift that same amount. The person who can move it faster is said to be more powerful. Moving weights quickly (i.e. explosively) also makes them feel lighter. Try picking a heavy dumbbell off a rack quickly and then do it again slowly, you will notice the difference immediately. Consequently, powerlifting is somewhat of a misnomer because speed is not taken into consideration – strength lifting would be more appropriate, but it does not sound as good! Unlike strength training regimes, which can be as simple as adding 2.5 kg to the barbell every time you train a particular lift and grinding out the reps, power training is a little more complicated. The current consensus is that intensity and volume influence power development more strongly than does frequency of training.

Compensatory acceleration training (CAT)

Compensatory acceleration training (CAT) involves dropping the weights of your main lifts to approximately 50–70% of your 1RM and banging out a few sets as fast as possible, several times per week. The aim is to produce the same force output with a light load as you would with a heavy load, where the weight is light enough to allow explosive speed, yet heavy enough to produce adequate force. CAT also targets the central nervous system and teaches it to respond for maximal power through recruitment and development of the maximum number of motor units possible, especially fast-twitch muscle fibres that are the bigger and more explosive muscle fibres in the body and the type used when pulling a 1RM. Performing more sets of fewer reps (three is a good number) works better than fewer sets of more reps.

This technique can be applied to all lifts, but take care because form and technique can be compromised when moving quickly and, of course, if you have altered your technique to perform the reps faster then there will not be an effective carry over to your 1RM attempt when using proper form. That said, you should not pause on the chest during bench press CAT. It is also important to make sure you are properly warmed up (CAT style) before you start.

Post-activation potentiation (PAP)

CAT can be further enhanced by applying the principle of post-activation potentiation (PAP), which serves as a means of maximizing acute power development. The basic concept is that force exerted by a muscle can be increased by forcing it to contract under a heavy load beforehand. Of course, too much volume would lead to fatigue, so the idea here is to use heavy loads for single reps. Essentially, excitation of the nervous system produces an increase in contractile function due to a heavy load stimulus. The optimum rest time between the heavy lift and the subsequent work set appears to be seven minutes. More research is required to fully understand this phenomenon, especially with regard to powerlifting training and whether it has a sustained effect or if it is purely short term. I have certainly found that working up to a heavy weight for a single rep makes my lower weight work sets feel easier.

For additional explosive lifts look at learning and including the Olympic lifts: snatch, clean and jerk, or derivatives thereof such as the power clean. Additional plyometric exercises (bodyweight or weighted) such as box jumps and burpees are also highly effective and serve as a means to bridge the gap between strength and power training methods.

The mind–muscle connection

If you have spent any time with bodybuilders then you will almost certainly have come across the idea of the mind–muscle connection. Simply put, the term refers to a conscious and deliberate muscle contraction, whereby a person is able to focus the tension created during exercise on a specific muscle or region of muscles in the body. Essentially, it is the difference between passively and actively moving a load.

When you employ the mind–muscle connection to create contractions, your brain recruits a greater percentage of muscle fibres to complete the task and also prevents innervating muscle fibres not in use. By creating tension in the right muscles, your body is better able to gain strength and size in all the right places. You will find some muscles easier to focus on than others. For example, who hasn't flexed their biceps in the past. You know this muscle well, you can see this muscle easily and therefore, it is easy to focus on it as you contract it. For other muscles where you are not able to generate such a strong mind–muscle connection so readily, a simple touch with a finger will help facilitate the process. By contrast, there are other muscles where it can be very difficult to generate a connection. For example, the *erector spinae* or spinal erector muscles in the lower back. There are several reasons for this. You have never seen them, you were probably unaware of them, and you have most likely never deliberately contracted them before. However, these particular muscles are very important for powerlifters and are easily damaged if overloaded, so it is important to become more aware of them.

Learning the compound lifts is similar to learning any complex task. For example, learning to drive will be familiar to many. You will no doubt recall having to concentrate on each element of the process separately until you became competent enough to complete the task of driving, whereby the entire process seems to flow smoothly without any conscious thought. This will be similar with regard to learning the big lifts.

All three competition lifts are actually rather complex movements and can be broken down into different stages, as explained earlier in the explanation on how to execute the lifts. To very briefly summarize, the lifts can be broken down as follows:

70

Squat – setting up under the bar, unracking the bar, walk out and set ready to squat, lowering the bar, raising the bar, re-racking the bar; bench press – setting up on the bench under the bar, un-racking the bar and set ready to start, lowering the bar, raising the bar, re-racking the bar; deadlift – setting up, lifting the bar to lock-out, returning the bar to the floor.

You will not be able to complete any of these lifts nice and smoothly from the outset. You will need to learn the individual elements of the lifts separately, before combining them together in a single fluid motion. During the learning process you will pass through four stages of competence in the following order:

1. Unconscious incompetence: An individual does not understand how to do something and does not necessarily realize this deficit.
2. Conscious incompetence: The individual has recognized their own incompetence and continues practicing to become better.
3. Conscious competence: The individual has now learnt how to do what is needed, but it still needs lots of concentration. It may be broken down into steps but there is still conscious involvement in executing the skill.
4. Unconscious competence: The individual has now had so much practice that the new skill has become second nature and can be performed easily and without the need for excessive concentration on the different elements that make up the task.

This will take time and practice. A sure sign of competence is when all reps of a set are conducted with correct form and all reps are consistent in terms of speed, bar path, etc. and there are mobile phone apps available to monitor these variables (e.g. BarSense).

What this highlights is that it is not just your muscles that you will be training. Regardless of what stage of competence you are at, your muscular activity is the result of impulses sent from your brain, through your central nervous system (CNS) via nerves to the muscles themselves, where chemical neurotransmitters are produced that cause the muscles to contract. As your training progresses and you increase the intensity of your lifts the CNS will need to work harder in order to stimulate the increased degree of muscle force required to move the heavier weights. Hence, training of the CNS does not stop once unconscious competence has been achieved and this is something to bear in mind as it can be a cause of fatigue later on.

Do you need a coach?

Throughout this volume you will see frequent reference to using a coach, but it is not obligatory and mostly comes down to personal preference. Are you confident that you can learn how to perform the lifts correctly by yourself and can you plan your training to break through plateaus and so continue to make steady progress? This is unlikely to be the case, but even if it is, employing a coach to teach you the lifts will speed up the process significantly and will help minimize the risk of injuring yourself during these early stages. A coach can be useful if you are too busy (or lack the knowledge) to manage your own lifting program. Having somebody tell you when to lift and what to lift will save you a significant amount of time and 'guesswork' once you have progressed beyond the initial linear progression stage (explained later).

A good coach will work closely with each of their lifters, usually on a 1:1 basis in order to help them develop and keep progressing in all three of their competition lifts. In addition to working on the physical aspects of lifting, they will also help with developing the appropriate mindset for success in both training and competing and will also guide their lifters through competition day and advise on attempt selection. Strangely enough, a coach will often be able to call a better attempt selection than the lifter themselves. A good coach will quickly spot small technical errors that may be impacting on your lifting efficiency and will also put a halt to form creep before it becomes a problem. Of course, a coach should also be able to motivate you and gives you somebody to be accountable to in terms of actually doing your training and pushing yourself hard enough to achieve your set goals.

If you decide to go down this route make sure your coach has real powerlifting experience. This may sound obvious but there are many regular Personal Trainers who profess to offer powerlifting coaching, but many of them will not teach you how to perform the lifts to competition standard because they have no idea what that actually entails. Some will have never competed or even attended a meet, so will be unable to help with first hand competition experience and will be just as confused as you are if you can manage to get them to support you at a competition.

British Powerlifting maintains an up-to-date regional list of qualified powerlifting coaches on its website. Alternatively, ask other powerlifters for recommendations. Check out their social media profiles, competition experience, etc. If you see somebody that appeals to you arrange to book in a single session with them to see how you get along. If you cannot find a suitable coach in your area or you train during anti-social hours then online coaching is another possibility. In this case your coach will send you a program for the week and you will need to record the lifts as you do them. Your coach can then assess your lifts remotely and provide technical feedback and your new routine for the following week.

Gym training fails

In most of the photographs throughout this book you will see that there is at least one spotter (often two or three) supporting the lifter during squats and bench press. Whilst it may not be immediately obvious that there is any similar assistance with the deadlift, there is usually a spotter lurking in the background ready to step up and provide assistance should the lifter become unstable on their feet.

The internet is replete with movie clips of would-be (and very experienced) lifters getting into all sorts of problems whilst attempting to lift heavy loads. These include squatters unable to get back up out of the hole and subsequently collapsing under the weight of the bar, bench pressers getting pinned down with the bar crushing their windpipe and deadlifters fainting and crashing to the floor following over-exertion with poor breathing technique. If you are particularly unfortunate any one of these can have catastrophic (or even fatal) consequences.

Therefore, in addition to learning how to conduct the lifts properly, it is also a very good idea to practice failing them with light weights, so that in the event you do fail with a heavy load and don't have a spotter helping out (and this will happen at some point!), you will be better able to deal with it safely. Indeed, safely exiting a lift gone wrong is as much of a required skill as mastering the correct technical move-ment of the lift itself.

The first and most obvious thing to state is that it is vital that you keep safety in mind at all times. Make sure your lifting area is clear and free of any trip hazards, such as gym bags, water bottles, log books, etc. and wherever possible if you are lifting without a spotter, squat and bench in a power rack with the safety bars set at an appropriate height. Even then failure is not without risk as fingers can get trapped between the heavily laden bar and the safety supports and if the bar has a particularly aggressive knurling it can make a serious mess of your digits. If you do fail, try to maintain balance to make sure you stay central and keep your hands away from the sides of the rack.

Safely failing the squat

If squatting in a power rack, lower the bar back down as much as possible then drop down on to your knees allowing the weight of the bar to be taken by the safety bars. Do not throw or drop the bar off your back as soon as you have realized you are going to fail the rep. It can hit you on the way down, damage the kit or injure other people in close proximity. If you are not squatting in a rack and have no choice but to discard the bar then lean back and drive the bar off your back while jumping forwards at the same time. If you do not move forwards quickly the bar is likely going to hit and scrape down your back and/or hit your lower back on the way down and it will not be pleasant. If it catches on your belt it can flip you over backwards and take you down with it! Whatever you do, DO NOT LEAN FORWARDS. The bar will roll over your neck and head on its way to the floor and will cause your body to buckle in a very awkward manner as it takes you crashing down with it.

There are some (very rare and unlikely) situations where you may fail a squat and have very little control over what happens next. For example, if you tear muscles or tendons, damage a vertebral disc, etc. you may find your only option is to collapse to the ground in pain. If you are inside a power rack the safety bars will save you from having to contend with additional injuries. The moral of the story, squat inside a power rack with the safety bars set to an appropriate height, which you can judge during your warm-up lifts.

Safely failing the bench press

Again, training in a power rack with the safety bars set at an appropriate height is the best way of avoiding most problems following a bench press failure. However, there will most likely be times when you need to train on a regular bench press set up without any safety bars or spotters. Indeed, some people train like this most of the time. The bench press is certainly the most dangerous of the lifts and mistakes can be fatal, although many fatalities could be avoided by following some simple rules. When lifting alone don't fix the weights on the bar using collars (or clips). In the event of a failed lift you will be unable to remove the plates from the bar and will remain pinned to the bench until somebody helps you remove the bar. If you are not using collars you should be able to tilt the bar to one side and allow some or all of the plates to slide off onto the floor. The bar will then flip back to the opposite side and the same thing will happen. This is not an ideal situation and lifting without collars can be problematic if the weights tend to slide along the barbell sleeves as you complete your reps. It also creates an added risk for other people (or pets if lifting at home) that may be in the immediate vicinity.

However, this should be seen as somewhat of a last resort. It is preferable that you do not allow the bar to come to rest and pin you down in the first place because when it touches your chest it will likely roll either towards your head or towards your feet. If it rolls towards your head you are in big trouble because it can crush your windpipe and asphyxiate you. For this reason you need to make sure you force the bar towards your legs using the so-called 'roll of shame' technique, assuming the bar is light enough to accomplish this and once you have practiced it a few times you will find that it is much quicker and easier than shaking the plates off the bar.

There are plenty of video tutorials online (YouTube), but in short what you do is keep calm and do not allow the barbell to fall or bounce on your chest, as this will only compound the problem by increasing the likelihood of additional injuries such as torn muscles or broken ribs. The best thing to do is raise your head and chest off the bench and roll the bar down your sternum, over your abdominals, and as it reaches your hip crease you can sit up, then stand up with the bar and RDL (Romanian deadlift) it down to the floor. This is a very quick manoeuvre and most people will not even notice that it is anything out of the ordinary unless they are watching you specifically.

Safely failing the deadlift

Trying to grind out a max deadlift gone wrong is never a good idea, even at competition. If the bar won't move any further and you find yourself in trouble, simply release your grip and let it fall to the floor. Jump backwards as soon as you let go of the bar in order to prevent the bar from hitting the top of your knees on the way down. If you pull using the sumo technique, make sure you bring your feet inward or collapse your stance in some way to avoid any chance of the plates landing on your toes (the barbell might bounce around a little after you drop it).

Competitive Powerlifting

Competing is about stepping out of your comfort zone and condensing all your previous months of training experience and progress into approximately five minutes on the platform over a period of several hours. It adds multiple new, external stress elements to your planning and lifting beyond what you would normally experience in regular training and provides a defined endpoint to focus on for this particular phase of your training. If you do decide to take this step (and you should) you will raise your lifting game to a higher level. Stepping out of your comfort zone is where true progress, both mental and physical, really happens.

Competing will not appeal to everybody and that is not a problem – each to their own. However, there is such a feeling of achievement and satisfaction once you have completed your first competition that you will almost certainly start planning your next one within a very short period of time. You may not appreciate what you are doing at the time as a result of being too preoccupied with everything that is going on, but I guarantee that after the event you will look back on it with awe and consider it a massive achievement.

I have coached a number of people up to and through their first competitions and knew that if I had suggested competing at the outset of their training they would have had no interest. However, a few months into their training I felt it better timed to broach the subject and although met with scepticism I knew I had planted a seed that I could nurture over the coming weeks. Ultimately they agreed that they wanted to compete so I got them registered for the meet. Their training was programmed accordingly and as we got closer to competition day they started to get more nervous and look for excuses to withdraw. Fortunately, I managed to keep them on track and also handled them at the competition. I have not yet come across anybody who did not enjoy the rush of their first competition.

Powerlifting competitions follow a standardized format, whereby each competitor is allowed three attempts on each of the lifts in the order: squat, bench press, deadlift, and their competition total is calculated by summing up the highest numbers for each of the different lifts, assuming those lifts were executed correctly. There are three referees, one central (who also gives the lifting commands) and two side refs,

one on either side of the lifter. Each referee judges the lift and presents a white light for a good lift and a red light for a failed lift. Two or more white lights count as a good lift. Two or more red lights count as a failed lift. The lifter must get a least one good lift in each of the three disciplines in order to obtain a 'total' and 'place' in the competition.

If a lifter happens to fail all three attempts of a specific lift they are said to have 'bombed out' of the competition. This tends to happen most often with new lifters who set their openers too high, on the expectation that because they can lift it easily in the gym, they will also be able to do it easily at competition. Be warned, this is not the case! However, it is not unknown for very experienced lifters to bomb out, even on the world stage, such as at international championship competitions. In this case, it is not the naivety of the lifter, but more likely they have misjudged how the stress of the event (possibly including air travel and sleeping in an unfamiliar place, unusual foods, etc.) have affected their ability to perform so close to the margins of their physical capability on that particular day. The mind can also play tricks on

Zahida Bibi stepping out of her comfort zone as a Masters 1 lifter at a non-sanctioned club competition, Warrington, 2023. Image credit FMX.

Non-sanctioned 'club' competitions are a great opportunity to find out if the sport is right for you, without having to make a substantial financial outlay on approved kit beforehand, Warrington, 2023. Image credit FMX.

lifters of all levels of experience, though this is less likely to be an issue with very experienced competitors. A general rule of thumb, often quoted, is that your opener for each of the lifts should be a weight that you can manage for a triple easily in the gym, even on a very bad day.

Ultimately, the aim is to lift as much weight as possible. For each age group and weight class, the lifter with the highest total wins. In many meets the lifter with the highest total relative to their weight class also wins. That is, the relative strength of all lifters is compared to determine the best overall lifter of the competition. If two or more lifters achieve the same total, the lighter lifter is ranked above the heavier lifter.

There are different competitions to accommodate the diverse range of lifters. Some are 'open' competitions in which anybody can enter, whereas others are single sex competitions, just for Masters lifters, Juniors (and Sub-Juniors), disabled lifters, university lifting clubs, novice lifters, etc. Some championship competitions require entrants to have secured a defined 'total' at a sanctioned competition within the year prior to the event. These totals can usually be found on federation

and divisional websites, and often on the competition information page. Novice competitions are a great opportunity for new lifters to get a taste of competition in a more relaxed environment where everybody else has a similar level of experience.

All the aforementioned are 'sanctioned' competitions and require that lifters use only approved brands and specific apparel and to be a member of the relevant governing federation. This, on top of the entrance fee, can amount to a considerable sum of money (ca. £200+), which is a rather significant outlay for somebody who may not be sure that competitive powerlifting is right for them. Fortunately, there has been a new initiative in recent years, referred to as a non-sanctioned 'club' competition. These are run under the same lifting rules as regular competitions, but participants need only pay a nominal registration fee (usually less than £20) and are able to use any brand of equipment, appropriate apparel, etc. There tend to be some 'rules' about how many of these you can do, and whether or not you are allowed to do them after you have already competed in a sanctioned competition, so do check with your local division, but they are a great way of getting platform experience, again, with people of a similar beginners-level of experience.

The author squatting at his first sanctioned (novice) competition, Liverpool, 2018. Notice how the hip crease is below the top of the knee, representing a competition-depth squat. There is no significant benefit in going any deeper than this, but it is important that you are not creating any degree of ambiguity for the referees, some of whom may not give you the benefit of the doubt if the depth is questionable. Image credit LD.

Squat

There are two types of competition squat depending on the equipment used: conventional stand and monolift stand. The former is called the walked out squat and the latter lift is referred to as the monolift squat. Not all federations allow for monolift squats, including the IPF, so it will not be considered further here.

Following "The Bar is Loaded" command, the lifter approaches the platform facing forwards towards the centre referee, sets up under the bar, lifts it off the rack and then steps back to his or her preferred position. The lifter needs to be standing erect with the feet flat on the floor, the knees locked-out and with the loaded bar resting horizontally across the lifter's shoulders and demonstrably under control before the referee will give the command to start the lift. The hands and/or fingers gripping the bar may not extend beyond the inside of the barbell collars – the lifter must not hold the collars or discs at any point during the execution of the lift.

The lifter must wait in this position until the head referee gives a signal consisting of a downward movement of the arm and audible command "Squat". The lifter then

The author squatting at his 13th sanctioned competition four and a half years later, North West Masters, 2022. The only real difference between this and the photo opposite is the position of the bar on the back: high bar squat in 2018 and low bar squat in 2022. Image credit FMX.

usually takes a deep breath and creates a break in the hips, bends their knees and drops into a squatting position until the hip crease is below the top of the knee. The lifter then returns to the erect starting position. The bar may slow to a stop on the way back up, but there must be no downward motion during the recovery phase of the lift. The lifter must wait for the referee to give the final signal, consisting of a backward motion of the arm and the audible command "Rack" and can then make a reasonable attempt to return the bar to the rack, assisted by the spotters if need be. This completes the competition squat.

The lifter may enlist the help of spotters in removing the bar from the rack, but once the bar has cleared the racks, the spotters are not allowed to physically assist the lifter in getting into the proper start position. The spotters may help the lifter maintain control should the lifter stumble or demonstrate any evident instability. At the referee's discretion, a lifter may be given an additional attempt at the same weight if a failed attempt was deemed due to an error by one or more of the spotters.

Many lifters will squat to depth and no further, but this can sometimes create a level of ambiguity given the very short time (fraction of a second) they remain in the hole

The author squatting 155 kg as a Masters 2 lifter at the All England Championships, 2022, showing the start position (opposite page) and the bottom of the lift below. The depth image is just on the mark and because it is only held for a fraction of a second may be considered questionable by some referees. If possible, it is a good idea to squat slightly deeper, just to avoid any ambiguity. Of course, if this is your opener and they give you the benefit of the doubt, you can be sure they will be watching your subsequent attempts very closely. Image credit WLM.

If you approach the bar with the belief that you can lift it, then in all likelihood you probably will. All England Championships, 2022. Image credit WLM.

and the fact that spotters or lighting may make observing the lowest position of the hip crease problematic for the side referees. You may get the benefit of the doubt the first time around but you can be sure the referees will remember to pay extra close attention to your depth the next time you step on the platform. So, if you can go just that little bit deeper to avoid any such ambiguity, then it will be in your interest to do so.

Reasons for being red lighted (failing the lift)

- Failure to observe the head referee's signals at the commencement or completion of the lift, i.e. if you start to descend before the "Squat" command or take a step forwards to rack the bar before the "Rack" command.
- Performing a double bounce at the bottom of the lift or taking more than one recovery attempt to rise up 'out of the hole'.
- Failure to assume an upright position with knees locked-out at the start or end of the lift.
- Moving the feet in a manner that would constitute a step or stumble, except when racking the bar. This includes resetting the feet after the "Squat" command.
- Failure to squat to sufficient depth, i.e. with the hip crease below the top of the knees.
- Spotters touching the bar between the referee's commands.
- Contact of elbows or upper arms with the legs.
- Failure to make a reasonable attempt to return the bar to the racks.
- Any intentional dropping or dumping of the bar. This is very dangerous for both the lifter and the spotters, but I have seen it happen!

Bench press

Following "The Bar is Loaded" command, the lifter approaches the platform and sets up with his or her back resting on the bench, head oriented towards the centre referee. The lifter takes the loaded bar and lifts it off the rack, positioning it over the chest with the arms locked-out straight. It is up to the lifter whether or not they do this entire process themselves or alternatively they can enlist help from either the centre or side spotters. If you have specific hand-off requirements make sure you clearly explain these to the hand-off person. For example, you may want them to lift the bar out from the rack after a 3-count (make sure it is you doing the counting) or when you nod your head. Likewise, you may want them to wait for a specific signal

The author setting up to lift at the British Bench Press Championships, 2021 – note the spotters and centre and side referees in the photo. Opposite page: The same competition showing the arms locked-out straight at the start (and end) of the lift (top) and the bar paused on the chest at the bottom of the lift (bottom) – note the position of the elbows relative to the shoulder (re: technical rule change as of January, 2023). Image credit WLM.

from you to indicate you are ready for them to release the bar under your control. It only takes a short moment to explain your requirements to the hand-off person when you step on the platform. If you wish to lift the bar out yourself also let the centre spotter know – a wave of the hand is usually enough and you will see him or her back off away from the bench. Using the two side spotters for a hand-off is not a good idea due to communication difficulties and the fact they are unlikely to both release the bar at exactly the same time which will result in balance problems from the outset.

If desired, the lifter may enlist the help of a personal spotter to remove the bar from the rack, but only designated spotters may remain on the platform during the lift. A designated spotter, having provided a centre hand off, must immediately vacate the area in front of the head referee and move to either side of the bar. If the personal spotter does not immediately leave the platform or impedes the head referees' responsibilities, the referees may decide to declare a "no lift" and give three red lights. Personal spotters must not return to the platform upon completion or failure of the lift and it is the responsibility of the lifter to make sure their personal spotter understands all of these obligations.

The bar must be gripped using a double-overhand grip, with the thumbs wrapped around the bar. Underhand or thumbless (suicide) grips are not permitted. The

spacing of the hands, as measured between the forefingers, must not exceed 81 cm, and the bar will have circumferential machine markings or tape indicating this maximum grip allowance. If for any reason a lifter needs to use an offset or unequal grip on the bar, where one hand will be placed outside the marking or tape, the lifter must explain this to the head referee, and allow inspection of the intended grip prior to making an attempt. Ideally, this will be done before the bench session commences or even better, before lift off. If it is not done until the lifter is on the platform for an official attempt, any necessary explanation and/or measurements will be done on the lifter's time for that attempt which will more than likely exceed the one minute allowance, and the lifter will be timed out and receive three red lights.

When the centre referee is happy that the lifter is in the correct position – head, shoulders and buttocks in contact with the bench surface and feet in flat and firm contact with the platform (or on raised blocks for shorter lifters) with an appropriate grip and the bar is under control, they will give the "Start" command.

The lifter then lowers the bar to the chest and pauses with the bar motionless and in contact with the body, but it must not touch the lifting belt if worn. At this point the underside of the elbow joints must be level with (or below) the top of the shoulder joints (new rule from January 2023). The referee then gives a "Press" command, whereby the lifter then pushes the bar back up to the starting position above the chest. The bar may move horizontally and may stop during the upwards phase of the lift, but is not allowed to move downward towards the chest. Once the arms are locked-out and the bar is motionless, the referee gives the "Rack" command and the lift is completed as the weight is returned to the rack, assisted by the side spotters if need be.

Reasons for being red lighted (failing the lift)

- Failure to observe the referee's signals from commencement through to completion of the lift.
- Raising the buttocks off the bench or any excessive movement or change of contact of the feet during the lift proper.
- Letting the bar sink into the chest after receiving the referee's "Press" command.
- Pronounced uneven extension of the arms during or at the completion of the lift.

- Any downward motion of the bar during the ascent phase of the lift.
- Spotters touching the bar between the referee's commands.
- Any contact of the lifter's shoes with the bench or its supports.
- Deliberate contact between the bar and the rack uprights during the lift with the intention of assisting the completion of the press.
- Failure to lower the underside of both elbow joints level with or below the top surface of each respective shoulder joint (new rule from 1st January 2023).

This last rule was implemented recently in order to stop the practice of hyper-arching and the consequent minimal range of motion lifting following numerous complaints having been received, specifically after the 2022 IPF World Bench Press Championships held in Almaty, Kazakhstan.

Deadlift

Following "The Bar is Loaded" command, the lifter walks onto the platform and up to the loaded bar which is resting on the floor. Facing the referee, the lifter grasps the bar in both hands, using one of a number of optional grips (double overhand, double overhand hook, alternate) and pulls the weights off the floor to assume an erect position with the knees locked-out, the shoulders back and the bar motionless. The bar may stop during the ascent, but there must be no downward motion of the bar. There is no initial command from the referee to start the lift! Once in the erect position, the head referee signals for the lifter to return the bar to the floor under control. This consists of a downward movement of the arm and the audible command, "Down". The bar must not be dropped. The IPF rules commission will be revising the technical rules for sumo deadlift in 2023.

Reasons for being red lighted (failing the lift)

- Any downward motion of the bar before it reaches the final lock-out position.
- Failure to stand erect with the shoulders back.
- Failure to lock the knees out straight at the top of the ascent.
- Supporting the bar on the thighs during the performance of the lift. 'Supporting' is defined as a body position adopted by the lifter that could not be maintained without the counterbalance of the weight being lifted.
- Movement of the feet that would constitute a step or stumble.
- Lowering the bar before receiving the head referee's command.
- Allowing the bar to return to the platform without proper control.

Opposite page: The author pulling 195 kg for his second attempt at the All England Championships, 2022, showing the deadlift locked-out at the top of the lift. Notice the knee-length socks which must be worn in order to prevent the possibility of blood from getting on the bar as it is pulled up the shins. If also wearing knee sleeves, these must not touch the top of the socks. Following the "Down" command from the referee, the bar must be returned to the floor under control. If you drop the bar you will get three red lights and a failed lift! Image credit WLM.

Spotting, loading and overcoming platform (stage) fright

You will soon come to realize that it takes a considerable number of people to run and manage a powerlifting competition safely and efficiently and competition organizers will welcome volunteers to fulfil the various roles. These include, table staff (to run software, record next attempts, answer general questions etc.), a MC, referees (at least three and possibly six if the competition is due to run all day), people to set up the venue ready for the competition (then take it back down again at the end), people to run the weigh-in and take the opening lifts, kit check, rack heights, door/entry staff, a runner for getting coffees, snacks, etc. and dealing with general bits and pieces, a photographer/live stream technician and finally the platform crew. The platform crew consists of a platform manager and two spotters and two loaders.

Spotters and loaders are important members of the crew that contribute to both the safety and efficiency aspects of the competition. In order for the competition to run smoothly, the correct plates need to be made ready for the next lifter as quickly as possible, resulting in the minimum possible amount of wasted time between lifts. If you have not done this before, do not worry, you will soon get into the swing of things. Make sure you have a drink and some snacks because once you are up there you are there for the duration, and this last point is why it can be of significant benefit to you. Many people get nervous when they first compete and it is their turn to step on to the platform. Indeed, it can take many competitions before a lifter overcomes this fear, which can be considered akin to stage fright. This is not really surprising given that although you may be at a competition for six to ten hours, you are actually likely to spend less than ten minutes of that on the platform! So, to get an hours worth of platform time would take six competitions!

If you volunteer as a loader or spotter you will get several hours of platform time at a single competition and you can use this to watch the lifters and the crowd and assess exactly what is going on. You will note that most of the time majority of the crowd are not scrutinizing the lifters. They may be chatting with each other, playing with their phones, whilst waiting for a friend to come up and lift, at which point they will pay attention and cheer them on. This will help you become more confident on the platform and it will pay dividends when you next step on it to lift. Be warned though, loading and spotting are both hard work, physically and mentally, especially if you are not used to steel competition plates. They are much more difficult to manoeuvre than regular gym tri-grip plates and if you happen to be loading for the

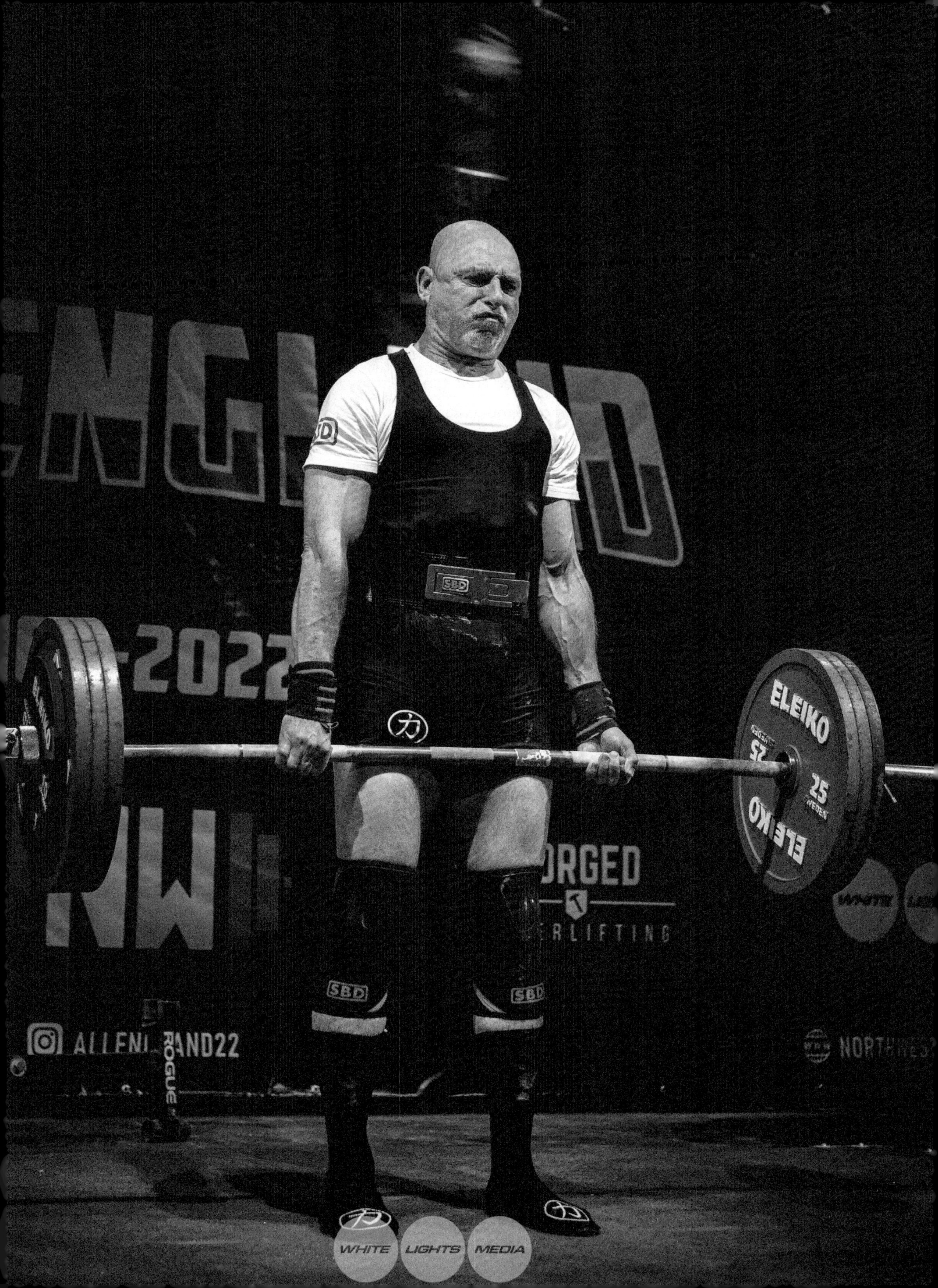
ELEIKO
25
SWEDEN
SBD
ROGUE
WHITE LIGHTS MEDIA

heavy lifters then you could be shifting lots of 25 kg plates. Usually, there will be just two or three spotters on the platform, but this increases to five for lifts of 200+ kg.

As a spotter you need to be ever vigilant because you literally have the life of the lifter in your hands. It is not a job to be underestimated or taken lightly (pardon the pun), but if you handle the bar or weights unnecessarily then you can cause the lift to be disqualified, so make sure you understand exactly what is expected of you before you start. In most instances when lifters fail attempts they are still able to handle the majority of weight on the bar and all that is required from the spotters is for them to take some of the weight and aid the lifter to get the bar back into the rack. However, on rare occasions the lifter may lose total control of the weight (e.g. due to back, muscle or tendon injuries during squats, the bar slipping out of the hands during the bench press or fainting during or after a deadlift) and it is here that you will be required to be quick and effective in order to prevent potentially serious injury to the lifter or yourself. You must remain focused and be prepared to respond quickly – the job is 99.9% boredom, 0.1% panic.

Spotters can also suffer serious (potentially career ending) injuries when lifters lose total control of the bar, as recently happened at a 2023 USA meet. A lifter bailed out (dumped the bar) from under a 285 kg squat, resulting in one of the spotters suffering one crushed and one seriously severed finger.

Volunteering is also a great way to get to know more people and help contribute to the sport and it may also help you secure your place at a future competition, now that there tend to be more lifters wanting to participate than there are lifting places available. Some divisions give previous volunteers preferential consideration when a new competition opens for entry. At the very least it is always a good idea to go and watch a competition before you do one yourself. Do this in person rather than watching it online as it will give you a feel for the atmosphere. Watch the lifters stepping on the platform and imagine yourself in their place. If you get the chance step up on the platform and have a brief look out at the crowd seating area. This will give you an even better feel for what competing might feel like. Obviously, you will need to do this when the platform is empty. There is usually a ten minute break between the different lifts, so you might get a chance to do it then. Alternatively, do it before the competition begins or once it has finished.

Deciding on your first competition

When should you do your first competition?

The best time to start competing is once you have a few months of experience executing all three lifts with correct form. Of course, you will not be competitive at this stage, but you will be getting extremely valuable competition platform experience that will be of great benefit to you when you do want to start pushing your numbers up. I have come across many people who have refused to start competing until they can hit a certain total in the gym. This may take several years or maybe won't even happen at all, and even if it does, the fact that they will have no previous competition experience means that things have more chance of going wrong on the day, especially when trying to hit big numbers.

The benefits of starting competing in the early stages of your training are numerous. You will get the feel for the great camaraderie amongst competitive powerlifters and will start to make many new friends. At each event you will no doubt make more friends and it will not be long before you are recognized as a regular. It is good to watch the technique of other lifters and also to have the possibility to benefit from chatting with more experienced lifters. Most importantly though you will have fun. You will develop confidence on the platform and become familiar with the commands and how the demands of competition day differ from training in the gym. This will put you in a better position to manage your competition day numbers further down the line when you want to be more competitive. This may give you the edge over the person who has waited to hit their gym total but who has zero competition experience!

How to find and register for your first competition

Whichever federation you choose to lift with will most likely have a web page with an events calendar, which will list the scheduled events for the coming year. It is worth checking this page frequently as sometimes additional competitions are added. The same holds true for the regional divisions within the federation. Each event should list the venue, date(s) and when the registration process will open (and close) for competitors. Most federations and divisions will provide competition updates via social media pages and some also via e-mail subscription services. Once you have decided on the competition you wish to do make sure you make a note of the opening date and time and try and register as soon as possible once

Start competing as soon as you can execute the lifts correctly. There is nothing to be gained by waiting until you can hit a certain total before you begin. It doesn't matter what you lift, it only matters that you lift and the platform experience that you gain from starting to compete early will pay dividends further down the line. Whatever you lift in your first competition will be a new comp PB whether it is a 200 kg total or a 500 kg total! Image credit FMX.

the competition has opened. It is not unusual for some of the smaller competitions to have sold out within half an hour. As extreme examples, I have seen a 50-place competition sell out within three minutes and a 180-place comp in a matter of seconds!

Some divisions have a priority registration arrangement for competitors who have volunteered to help at a recent competition and, as mentioned elsewhere in this book, it is a really good idea for you to do this in order to get a feel for how a competition runs and to familiarize yourself with the competition environment. If you really want to compete but all the slots in your divisional competitions have been filled it might be possible to lift as a 'guest' in a different regional division.

In order to register you will need to supply your federation membership number, your name, age, bodyweight class and pay the entry fee. If appropriate you may also need to supply your qualifying total and the date and competition at which it was achieved. The entry process normally opens 6–8 weeks before the competition. If you are unsure of which weight class you will be in ahead of time do not worry, you can change this up until about two weeks before the competition, but if you think you may need to do this check the cut off date and make a note of it.

Setting your competition goals

As with anything, if you set your own criteria for success, rather than blindly following the expectations of others, you will almost certainly come away with a win! For your first competition, your self-designated criterion for success might be stepping on the platform, especially if you are nervous about performing in front of others. Achieve this goal and you leave a winner, regardless of the weights you lift.

You can also set yourself a second goal of 'placing' in the competition, which means getting at least one good lift in each of the events: squat, bench press and deadlift. This will also give you a competition total, which will serve as a baseline for future competitions. It does not matter how small this total is, if it is your first competition then it will be a new competition personal best (PB) for you.

Goals may include leaving with a new PB on a specific lift, on all lifts, or on your competition total. You may aim for nine good lifts out of nine, but in my opinion, this is not necessarily a great goal in the latter stages of your competitive journey. Your goal may be a regional or national qualifying total (QT) for a subsequent event, a place on the podium (finishing in the top three) or may even be breaking an existing record at your particular age and weight class.

The more flexible you are with your goals for competition day the better, and the more likely you are to leave happy and content. If you just have a single goal that

you fail to achieve, then it will not be a good day for you. The key is to choose your numbers according to what you need, not what you would like. For example, if you need a QT for an upcoming competition there is nothing to be gained by trying to hit a new PB and failing at both as a result. I have seen this happen!

Regardless of your goals, you will need to start your preparation several months out. This will involve preparing a training program with the aim of peaking at your desired numbers on meet day. This will take some practice and you will get better at it as you become more experienced.

Competition formats

As mentioned previously, the best bet is to register for a non-sanctioned 'club'-type competition (or two), followed by a dedicated novice meet in order to ease yourself

The author at the North West Masters Championships, 2022, pulling 200 kg on the platform for the first time and a new competition PB. This was smashed approximately 10 minutes later with a good lift at 205 kg. Image credit FMX.

into the sport. However, there may be other considerations that need to be taken into account. For example, for various reasons, not everybody will be able to (or want to) execute all three lifts to competition standard and so they may wish to enter a single or double lift event, rather than a full power (three-lift competition).

Example meet formats include:
- Full Power: squat, bench press and deadlift
- Bench-only: bench press
- Deadlift-only: deadlift
- Push/Pull: bench press and deadlift

These may be further classified as follows:
- Raw (classic): Knee sleeves (sometimes wraps), belt and wrist wraps only
- Equipped: Specialty squat, bench, and deadlift suits are used

Most competitions open for registration at least eight weeks prior to the event and the places get filled up very quickly (sometimes within minutes), so you need to be organized. You will need to provide your age and weight class in addition to your federation membership number and payment. If applicable you may also need to provide your qualifying total with the date and event it was obtained.

In most cases it is possible to make weight class changes up until a couple of weeks before the competition, but after this if you do not weigh-in within the class parameters you have chosen, you will not be able to place in the competition. You may be allowed to lift as a 'guest' in the weight class you have fallen into, but even if you lift the most weight on the day, you will not get the kudos for having done so. Part of the discipline of powerlifting is being able to weigh-in correctly on the day. To begin with it is a good idea to select a weight class that you fall into comfortably, rather than trying to cut weight at the last minute to make the weight class. This is more the ambit of highly competitive lifters, who aim to train above the top limit of their weight class and cut below it for weigh-in, then refeed to be above it again, before the lifting begins. Whilst this can give them a slight edge over other competitors it is a risky business and sometimes they do not make the weight on the day! I have seen this happen on several occasions. Moreover, it is ill advised for novice lifters to cut weight prior to their first few competitions, as they are likely to be less competitive as a result.

It is a good idea to have some knowledge of your normal daily bodyweight fluctuations especially if you sit close to either the lower or upper-bound limits of a particular weight class. I record my weight daily as soon as I get up and have been to the loo, but I certainly don't stress myself if I am not within my expected range every single day. Always weigh yourself at the same time as it is surprising how much your bodyweight can fluctuate throughout the course of the day. For example, I can lose more than 2 kg just sleeping for nine hours!

Depending on which federation you lift with and the size and nature of the event, the weigh-in and gear check may fall anywhere between 24 hours to just a couple of hours before stepping onto the platform. Many people avoid eating or drinking prior to the weigh-in, but I prefer to maintain my regular routine, so try and make sure I have a couple of kgs safety margin on the morning of the event.

The different federations discussed earlier have slightly different rules, so it is important to make sure you are familiar with all the requirements well in advance of the event. These even include the type of underwear that is allowed, as some styles are not! For sanctioned competitions, only approved kit can be used and checks do take place at National level meets. Lists of approved items and their manufacturers should be available on the websites of the various federations. These requirements may not be so strictly enforced at local, regional or charity events, but don't rely on this. Approved kit tends to be somewhat more expensive, but it is worth purchasing this at the outset ... 'buy once, cry once', as the saying goes! Some online shops, e.g. StrengthShop indicate if an item is IPF-approved. If you are sure of your commitment to competing you might want to invest in a top quality belt (e.g. SBD) from the outset, which by itself can set you back close to £200 but is well worth the investment, as you will no doubt end up buying one eventually anyway.

Quiet competitions and focus zones

Regular powerlifting competitions are noisy events. The loud (often heavy metal) music, cheering crowd and the MC combine to generate a rather raucous cacophony, which for many lifters (including the author) has great appeal and serves to motivate the lifters to push to their limits. However, such an atmosphere is not for everybody and there are some lifters who would love to give competitive powerlifting a try, but for whom such an environment would make them feel too anxious and nervous.

A new 2023 initiative by North Midlands Powerlifting in collaboration with mental awareness partner Shawmind is to run a quiet competition series to IPF standards but without any of the hype typical of regular competitions. The competition would have no central platform, no bright lights, no loud music and no MC and would be conducted in a regular gym, with lifts judged and totals recorded and registered as per any other sanctioned competition. Lifters have the opportunity to raise any individual concerns prior to formally registering for the event. The first event took place in March 2023 and by all accounts was very successful.

Another aim is to have dedicated spaces, known as 'Focus Zones,' at competitions where lifters can get away from the hustle and bustle and focus their mind on the lifts ahead. This program will be run in conjunction with British Powerlifting's Safeguarding Officers, and the Focus Zone will be staffed by a volunteer trained in mental health awareness available to talk to about how you are feeling on the day, should you wish to do so. Alternatively, you can just use the space to chill out quietly for a bit. They will be trialled first by the North Midlands division before rolling them out further afield. There will also be Focus Zone contact cards around the meet venue, which will feature a QR-code that links to online additional coaching and well-being resources that may be of value to lifters.

The day before the event

The most important thing to do the day before you compete is to relax and make sure all your preparation is in order. Do not eat anything that is likely to upset your stomach and certainly do not eat any foods you are not used to for the same reason. Avoid alcohol and if possible go to bed a little earlier and get a good night's sleep. If you are prone to cramps it is a good idea to take an electrolyte drink before you go to bed (there is no harm in doing this for several nights up to comp day). The last thing you need is for your sleep to be rudely broken by excruciating calf cramp, which can also have a lingering impact into the competition itself.

Double check your travel arrangements to make sure there are no train cancellations or road closures, etc. and if travelling by car make sure you know in advance what the parking arrangements are and have some loose change available in case you need it for the car park.

It is advisable to visit the competition website and double check which flight you are in and your weigh-in time, as last minute changes are not unheard of. Make sure your kit bag is fully checked and packed (including your federation membership card if not stored digitally on your phone). The following checklist will help, but add to this anything else you may wish to take. The less faffing around you have to do on the day of the event the better.

- BP membership card / anti-doping confirmation e-mail
- Photo ID incorporating age or date of birth
- Singlet
- T-shirt(s)
- Lifting shoes (you may have several pairs, e.g. deadlift slippers)
- Long socks (for deadlift)
- Knee sleeves / wrist wraps (if using)
- Medical tape and scissors (if using for hook grip – check your federation rulebook to make sure it is approved! It is OK for IPF)
- Belt (if using)
- Chalk / talc / smelling salts / gum shield (if using)
- Foam roller / resistance bands / skipping rope, etc. for warming up
- Music / headphones, etc.
- Food / drinks (including pre-workout, re-hydration electrolytes, etc.)
- Money (for snacks, drinks, parking, competition t-shirts, etc.)
- Pen
- Plasters (we have all nicked ourselves in the gym generating cuts that refuse to stop bleeding. You really don't need this extra hassle on comp day, so be prepared just in case!)
- Toilet roll (depending on the venue, it can run out rather quickly!) and you might also find flushable wipes can come in handy!
- Absorbent pantie liners (if you are prone to leaking when lifting heavy)
- Bench press blocks (if you use them and they conform to the required specifications)

Having a physical checklist, as above, can also be useful when packing up your kit at the end of the competition. Because my competition bag contents are different from my training bag contents I always make a concerted effort to make sure that I know where everything is, so that when I get to the competition venue I will be able to find whatever I am looking for with ease. It never, ever works out like that and within minutes of opening my bag the whole order of things is in disarray. That is just the way it is. At large events, lots of lifters means lots of bags all containing very similar kit. Take time to make sure you pack up everything and that everything you do pack actually belongs to you. You don't want to travel two hours to get home and find you have two left-foot shoes and no right-foot shoe or that you have forgotten to pack your £200 lifting belt! It does happen!

What happens on the day?

Getting to the event

The first order of the day is getting yourself and your kit to the event in time to make the weigh-in. I always aim to arrive early in order to mitigate against any unexpected travel disruption (a train journey to my first novice competition that should have taken 30 minutes took over two hours, but I still made the weigh-in ... just!). If you are flying to the event make sure you take all your kit on as cabin baggage – wear it if need be, including your belt! If all your competition gear goes in the hold and happens to get lost, as does happen, then you will not be happy and will most likely be unable to compete.

If possible have somebody drive you to the event so you do not need to worry about getting home, particularly if it is a long journey. There are several times I have travelled to a competition by train and at the end of the event was very happy that I did not need to drive myself home. You can also get your driver to take photos and record your lifts in the event that the organizers are not already doing this. Sometimes there are professional photographers documenting the event and photo-packages can be ordered in advance when you register to lift or after the event.

On the occasions I have taken my young kids I have found them to be a major distraction, so I would advise against this. If you travel to the event by public transport try and book an 'open' ticket for your return journey. Competitions can sometimes run over by several hours and the last thing you want is to be worrying about missing your pre-booked train!

The first thing to do when you arrive is take a look around and familiarize yourself with the set-up. Find the weigh in room, the toilet facilities, warm-up areas and the main competition platform. Go and stand on the platform and look out at the seating area for the crowd and at the chair where the centre referee will be sitting and issuing the various lift commands. Visualize the crowd and the referee and get yourself comfortable with the idea of being on display and listening out for the commands.

Also, make a note of where you will be entering and exiting the platform (these may be different) and work out the best route to get to the control table in order to submit your next lift attempt without getting in the way of spotters, loaders, other lifters, referees etc. A multi-flight (and in some cases multi-platform) competition can create a very confusing environment for new competitors, so getting a feel for the place early on will help you when the competition starts. If you are unsure about anything ask. You will find most people are happy to assist you.

Weighing in

Once at the venue, you will need to weigh-in, where you will also be asked to show proof of valid federation membership, maybe also proof of age, and also to provide your openers (the first attempts) for each of your three lifts. This is something that you should have considered well in advance, so there should be no wasting time thinking about it when there is a huge queue of other lifters also waiting to weigh-in. Each of your openers should be an easy lift in order to secure a place in the competition and prevent you from bombing-out, as discussed earlier. You will normally have the option to alter your openers up until shortly before your lifting flight is due to commence. Remember, once you have selected a weight for a lift you cannot choose a lower weight for any subsequent attempt. You must either match a failed attempt or increase the lift by a minimum of 2.5 kg, so it is absolutely imperative that you make your openers nice and easy. You will most likely receive a book of attempt slips at weigh in, with which to communicate each of your next lift attempts to the table staff, once you have completed your previous lift attempt.

You may also be asked to sign (or show email evidence of electronic signature) a form agreeing to drug testing, and of course must conform should a designated tester request a sample from you at the event. You may also be asked for your bench press hand-off preference (e.g. centre hand off, side hand off, no hand off).

At some competitions weigh-in will be conducted in strict order, according to a list of names, usually attached to the door of the weigh-in room. If you miss your slot then you may need to wait until the end. At other competitions weigh-in is done on a first-come, first-served basis. Regardless, it will be in your interest to be present and available at the start of the weigh-in procedure. Normally I strip down to just my briefs and socks (for hygiene reasons) before standing on the scales. If you feel uncomfortable with this idea then it is also OK to weigh-in fully clothed, but you are of course reducing your competitive edge by doing so.

If you are late and miss the weigh-in then you will not be allowed to lift. If you do not weigh-in within the limits of the weight class you registered for then you will be classed as having not made weight. You may still be allowed to lift, but it will be in the weight class you weighed in at and it will be as a 'guest' lifter. You will not place in the final competition results. If you don't make weight you should be given the option to come back just before weigh-in closes to try again. Hopefully you will have managed to adjust your weight accordingly in the intervening period, assuming the discrepancy was not too great to begin with.

Consent to drug testing (anti-doping)

British Powerlifting is opposed to drugs in sport, strictly adheres to the IPF and the WADA (World Anti-Doping Agency) code and is the only powerlifting organization in the UK to undertake WADA approved independent drug testing. All lifters should be prepared to sign a consent form confirming their willingness to co-operate in any requests for samples. If paper forms are used these may be requested at weigh-in, but more recently electronic submissions ahead of time have come into operation, though you may still be expected to show a confirmation email.

Any member of British Powerlifting may be called upon for drug testing at any time, including at divisional championships. Lifters are not permitted to leave the venue of a sanctioned competition before the awards ceremony for their designated session and doing so without permission may result in disciplinary action. It is important that you read and understand the rules on testing, including where and when you can be tested (e.g. outside of competition – all members of British Powerlifting remain subject to the Anti-Doping Rules for a minimum of 12 months from the date they joined or their last competition, whichever is the later) or for how to go about getting a Therapeutic Use Exemption for medications you may be taking for health reasons. For more and up-to-date information see the relevant pages on the GB Powerlifting website (https://www.britishpowerlifting.org/anti-doping).

People do get caught every year and they are named (and shamed) in the testing summaries on the British Powerlifting website and via British Powerlifting 'News Update' emails. An anti-doping rule violation in connection with an in-competition test automatically leads to disqualification in that competition with all resulting consequences, including forfeiture of medals, points and prizes. Lifters can also receive a ban on competing for up to four years, or in the most extreme cases they can receive a lifetime ban.

Kit check

Weigh-in may (or may not) be followed by a kit check, to make sure everything you intend to use is of the correct specification and/or by an approved manufacturer. The following items may be checked: singlet, shoes (can be different for squat, bench and deadlift), belt (various specifications including both lever and prong buckles, but must be of an approved make), knee sleeves (or wraps), wrist wraps, t-shirt (plain cotton with sleeves that cover the delts), socks (knee length socks are required for the deadlift in order to prevent the possibility of bleeding from the shins on to the bar) and underwear.

Any items deemed inappropriate or considered to be unclean or torn will be rejected at this time and you will have the option of re-submitting alternative items. Throughout the competition the Technical Controller will also examine personal equipment worn by lifters in the warm-up areas and reject any items not conforming to the specifications of the technical rules. It is the responsibility of the lifter to ensure that all items to be worn on the platform have passed the scrutiny of the examining referees. If a lifter goes onto the lifting platform and/or performs a competitive lift wearing an inappropriate item of Personal Equipment that has not been checked-in they may be subject to penalty, e.g. disqualification of the last attempt.

If any referee has reason to question whether a lifters kit conforms to the required standards they will inform the Chief Referee of their suspicions following completion of the lift. The president of the Jury may then examine the kit in question. If the lifter is deemed to be deceitfully wearing or using any illegal item they shall be immediately disqualified from the competition. However, if the illegal item was passed in error during kit check, and the lift in which the discovery was made was successful, the lift will be rejected and the lifter will be permitted a new attempt (having removed the illegal item) at the end of the round.

If you are unsure about an item of your kit contact one of the event organizers beforehand, as there may be no opportunity to resolve problematic issues on the day. In other instances there may be approved sponsors selling kit at the event, so you might be lucky and still get to lift.

Rack heights

Following weigh-in and kit checks, you will be required to provide your rack heights for both the squat and the bench press. This is where you practice your set-up on a bit of competition spec kit to determine what height you need it to be set up at in order for you to be able to lift the bar off comfortably. You will most likely not be wearing your competition kit at this stage, but it is important to make sure you are wearing your squat shoes when you determine the rack height for this lift.

Most powerlifters tend to train on the same equipment day in and day out and once they have found their ideal rack height in the gym they do not really give it a second thought. They know exactly where the j-hooks need to be placed in the power rack in order to set the bar at their preferred height. Hence, when it comes to setting your rack height at competition it may feel a little odd that you have to think about this and you may find yourself faffing around raising and lowering the stands in order to get the bar at what you presume to be your ideal height. Given there will be a line of people behind you waiting to do the same thing, you may feel under pressure to rush the process and end up with your squat opener, moreover, your first lift of the competition set at a height that does not really feel right for you. A useful tip is to bring a tape measure and set your initial rack height based on the distance of the bar from the floor rather than how it feels or looks. Of course, you will need to know this same distance in your training facility set up for this to be of any benefit.

It is worth noting that you will be giving your rack heights using an empty bar, and that a heavily laden bar may actually sit slightly lower on the platform. If the rack height feels awkward on your first lift you should ask the table staff to have it raised for your subsequent attempts when you submit your second squat attempt weight.

When establishing your bench rack height you will also be able to ask for blocks to rest your feet on if you have short legs and you can also discuss any lift-off prefer-ences you have. Most people opt for a central lift-off, but you may prefer to have the side spotters do it or even to lift the bar off yourself. For some competitions your rack heights (if known) and openers are submitted online ahead of competition day.

Once this is done you can relax for a bit and maybe have a drink and eat some food as lift off should still be at least an hour away. Once all the lifters have weighed in and provided their opening lift attempts, these will be entered into the competition computer and screens showing these data should be available to view. It is very important that you check that your openers have been entered correctly, as the last thing you want is to find yourself expected to shift a weight 20 kg above what you had submitted. It is also a good opportunity to see what your competitors have chosen to open at, in order to help strategize your subsequent attempts if the competition looks like it is going to be close run thing.

Warming up

It won't be too long before you need to start warming up for your squats. If you are lucky there will be a separate, designated warm-up area incorporating competition spec kit and station crew to help with loading, spotting and changing rack heights for you. In smaller venues, such as local gyms, you may find yourself warming up with bumper plates, using non-comp-spec benches and squat racks. In either case, there will be far more lifters than there will be warm-up stations, so you will need to share the equipment and incorporate this requirement into your timings. What may take you 15 minutes in the gym may now take 40 minutes sharing with several other lifters. When choosing who to share with look for lifters of a similar size/body proportions to you, so there is no need to mess about unloading the bar to change rack heights between each lifter. Anything that wastes time or energy unnecessarily at a powerlifting competition is a bad idea.

You do not want to warm-up too early nor do you want to be rushing at the end, so make sure you keep a close eye on the time. However, it is extremely important that you always leave yourself sufficient time to change your opening attempt if your warm-ups are feeling more difficult than you expected. As you are warming up, you should be asking yourself if you are on track for the opening weight you provided at weigh-in. If not, you have the option to change it, but only up until a few minutes before the lifting starts and this is something I have done at several competitions. If you miss this deadline because you are still warming up it can be disastrous and even lead you to 'bomb out' right at the very start of the competition. This is not something I have done, but I have seen it happen. Even if you don't bomb out, but manage to grind out a difficult opener, this can have deleterious consequences for your confidence for the remainder of the competition.

Everybody has a slightly different warm-up routine during their regular training. Some people like to really get their heart pumping and blood circulating doing a quick burst of cardio on a bike, rower or something similar. Others incorporate mobility work to loosen off tight muscles and connective tissues in order to increase

The warm-up room at the All England Championships, 2022.

range of motion, e.g. to reach squat depth, or to loosen lats to facilitate squat set up. Other lifters may make do with dynamic or static stretching and/or muscle activation routines to focus on warming up the stabilizing muscles, which are not directly involved with shifting the load, but instead work to control the bar and restrict inefficient movement patterns, e.g. rotator cuffs, rear delts and lats for the bench press. During normal gym training, your warm-up can be as elaborate and time consuming as you like, but you need to be prepared to be flexible at competition venues where time and kit availability will be very limited.

It has been shown experimentally that a short period of isometric core training (e.g. planks, bird-dog, abs roll outs, etc.) will cause the trunk to remain stiff for a limited period of time afterwards. This will prime your core muscles for maintaining spinal stabilization prior to conducting squats and deadlifts both in regular training and on competition day. It is not clear how long this effect lasts, but you should aim to do this before your squat warm-ups and again before your deadlift warm-ups.

It is vitally important to make sure you don't wear yourself out, so there is no need to bang out too many reps during your main lift warm-ups. Some light mobility work followed by five minutes of isostatic core engagement, then a few reps at lighter weights, finished off by singles at heavier weights with a focus on competition standard technique should suffice. As a general rule I usually warm-up with decreasing increments. That is, the amount I increase on the bar gets lower as I work towards my opener. For example, here is a hypothetical warm-up and attempt schedule for an upcoming competition.

Squat	Bench press	Deadlift
40 kg – 8 reps	Bar only – 8 reps	60 kg – 8 reps
60 kg – 6 reps	40 kg – 6 reps	100 kg – 4 reps
80 kg – 4 reps	60 kg – 4 reps	140 kg – 3 reps
100 kg – 2 reps	80 kg – 2 reps	160 kg – 1 rep
120 kg – 1 rep	100 kg – 1 rep	180 kg – 1 rep
135 kg – 1 rep	110 kg – 1 rep	190 kg – opener
145 kg – 1 rep	115 kg – 1 rep	200 kg – 2nd attempt (new PB)
152.5 kg – opener	120 kg – opener	205 kg – 3rd attempt (new PB)
157.5 kg – 2nd attempt (new PB)	125 kg – 2nd attempt (new PB)	
162.5 kg – 3rd attempt (new PB)	127.5 kg – 3rd attempt (new PB)	

In a two-flight competition (i.e. the lifters have been split into two equal-sized groups: A and B) it will be time to start warming up for your bench press as soon as your competitive squat session has finished, and likewise your deadlifts as soon as your competitive bench press has finished. Two-flight competitions are rather intensive as you can find yourself non-stop powerlifting for two or three hours. In a three-flight competition (A, B, C), group A will get to have a rest after they have lifted, while group B is lifting and group C is warming up. Group A then starts to warm-up when Group C lifts and Group B rests. Once you are warmed up you should be good to go and it won't be long before you are due to step onto the platform and do your stuff!

Write down your planned warm-up schedule so that it is one less thing to think about on the day. It will also avoid you building up too much fatigue through getting carried away. Have a plan and stick to it!

The warm-up room is also a great opportunity to chat with people and make new friends. As of December 2022, the By-Laws of British Powerlifting were amended to specify that only British Powerlifting members are allowed in the warm-up areas for British and National Championship competitions. It was recognized that this may not be practicable for some non-national events and so was only made a recommendation for lower-level competitions. Following some debate, it was agreed (2023) that a discounted (non-lifting) membership for coaches would be introduced.

Example of an electronic score sheet at a three-flight competition – The All England Championships, 2022.

Example of an electronic score sheet at a two-flight competition – North West Masters Championships, 2022.

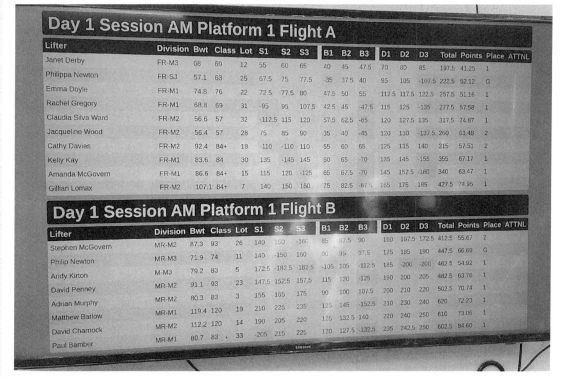

Managing your time

The venue may be anything from a relatively small gym for local competitions, to a large hotel, sports hall or other large venue for national or international events. Regardless, prepare yourself for a long day of heavy lifting if you are doing a full power, three-lift event! Flights are usually split into approximately equal sizes in order to give all competitors a similar amount of rest between lifts. Nonetheless, with highly efficient platform crew and organization the time between individual lifters stepping on the platform and completing their lifts can be less than one minute, such that in a flight of ten to twelve lifters, you may have just nine or ten minutes rest between your attempts, so make sure you don't wander off and make sure you keep a close eye on proceedings as you will be required back on the platform before you know it.

Flights can proceed even quicker if many of the lifters are making the same weight attempts, as there is no time wasted in changing plates on the bar. It is also important to understand that just because you were the third lifter on the platform for the first attempts round, does not necessarily mean you will be the third lifter for the subsequent attempts rounds because all following listings will depend on the new weights submitted by the lifters after their previous lift, which does have the potential to affect the running order. Again, you need to keep a close eye on the score sheet and listen to the announcements from the MC otherwise you could very easily miss your slot.

In a three-flight competition you may have approximately 70 minutes between each of your different lifts, i.e. between stepping off the platform from your last squat and stepping back on it for your first bench – and likewise between your last bench press and first deadlift. Consequently, you may find yourself lifting for in excess of four or five hours, including the warm-up. By contrast, if you are just doing a single-lift event, such as a bench only competition, you may find yourself having completed the competitive element within less than 20 minutes!

Once all the lifting has been completed you will need to hang around a short while longer for the awards ceremony. The platform will be cleared while the table staff make sure they have all the lift data collated accordingly so that they can release the final results, including the overall best lifters of the competition. The awards process can take some time at large competitions as there are separate awards for males and females, approximately eight different weight classes for each gender,

The competition platform at the All England Championships, 2022.

The competition platform, warm-up (the power racks) and spectators areas at the North West Masters Championships, 2022.

which can be further multiplied by the number of different age classes (e.g. Sub-Junior, Junior, Senior, Masters 1,2,3 and 4).

There are usually two best lifter awards, one for men and one for women. The best lifters are determined based on the IPF GL Points system (https://www.powerlifting.sport/fileadmin/ipf/data/ipf-formula/IPF_GL_Coefficients-2020.pdf). Once everything is ready all the lifters are called back to the platform/stage area for the awards ceremony where medals and/or trophies are distributed. These are normally awarded only to the top three lifters in each weight (and sometimes age) category who are called up to the podium one at a time in the order: bronze, silver, gold. At some competitions participation medals are also awarded to all the lifters.

It will be tiring and challenging, but it will also be fun and highly rewarding once you have completed it. I do not know anybody who did not enjoy their first competition. Indeed, most people seem to experience an unusual state of euphoria after their first few competitions. I know I did!

The author with a participation medal and 2nd place trophy at the British Bench Press Championships, 2021. Image credit WLM.

What weights should you attempt to lift?

This is the all important question! First, let's have a look at the rules. A lifter is permitted one change of weight on the first attempt of each lift, so long as this is done in the permitted time frame as announced by the MC. The change of weight may be higher or lower than that originally submitted at weigh-in.

No changes can be made to second or third attempt submissions for the squat and bench press. In the third round of the deadlift, two changes are permitted. The change of the weight may be higher or lower than the lifters previously submitted third attempt. However, these are only permitted provided that the MC has not already called the lifter to the bar already loaded to his previously submitted weight.

A lifter must submit their second and third attempts within one minute of completing their preceding attempt, with the one minute count starting when the results lights are activated. If no weight is submitted within the one-minute time frame, the lifter will automatically be given a 2.5 kg increase on their next attempt, the minimum allowed. If the lifter failed his or her previous attempt and did not submit a next attempt weight within the one-minute time frame, then the bar will be loaded to the failed weight for their subsequent attempt. Note, it is considered courteous to submit a formal attempt to the table crew even if you wish for your attempt weight to remain the same.

In IPF recognized competitions, the weight of the barbell must always be a multiple of 2.5 kg. Unless attempts are made on records, in squat, bench press and deadlift, the increment must be at least 2.5 kg between all attempts. In a record attempt the weight of the barbell must be at least 0.5 kg in excess of the current record and fractional micro-plates will be available to make these smaller weight increments.

So, how should you apply these rules to your competition day strategy? The most important thing is to make your openers nice and easy. The general rule of thumb is to select a weight that you can confidently manage for a triple in the gym, even on a bad day. For a first-time competitor I would suggest taking this approach and then subtracting another 10 kg just to be on the safe side. Having easy openers allows you to get a feel for the bar and rack setup and the judges' expectations with regards to timing of the commands (e.g. a short or long bench pause can make a big difference), and implementation of the rules (e.g. squat depth requirements, etc.)

without having to risk too much in terms of failing the lift. The most important thing to do at your first competition is score a total and that means getting at least one good attempt for each of the three lifts.

There are all sorts of reasons why competition lifting is different from training and why what you might hit in the gym relatively easily, you will fail at competition. Your squat first attempt needs to be easy because you have no idea how you will react the first time you step on the platform. Nerves will kick in whether you expect them to or not and jelly legs will effect the effectiveness of your squat ... so keep it light! Your bench press first attempt needs to be easy because, in addition to the fatigue from having done squats and your nerves, you have no idea how long the referee will make you pause with the bar on your chest. Some referees have a longer pause than others and this can be a real strength sapper. Use your warm-up to make sure you are on track to a confident two-count pause and if not change your opener! Your deadlift opener needs to be easy because by the time you get around to it you will have already been lifting at your max capacity for several hours. Again, use your warm-ups to check if you are still on track for the opener you presented at weigh-in and if not, change it.

As you gain more competition experience you will develop a better understanding of this and how your body reacts to each of the different lifts, but for your first competition PLAY IT SAFE! Any total you get, no matter how small, will be a new competition PB and something for you to build on next time. Remember, if you fail all attempts of a particular lift then you will 'bomb out' and not place (or be credited with a total) in the event. If you get a total you will leave happy, if you don't you won't!

You should have a plan of action well before the competition and make the final decision about your openers and expected subsequent attempts before competition day. Present your openers at weigh-in. Use your warm-ups to judge your abilities on the day and adjust your openers if needed. Use your preceding lifts to judge what you think is reasonable to hit on your subsequent attempts, as per your original plan. Use your second attempt to get your total up and aim to hit a new PB with your third. Once you have gained more competition experience you can open slightly heavier and aim to hit a new PB on your second attempt, followed by a second PB with your third. This is the approach I sometimes use and you can see my results in the tables on pages 137–138. Some coaches advise against aiming for a small PB on your second attempt in favour of a larger PB on your final lift. There is no hard and fast rule, but if you fail on your second attempt (as well as your third) then you will end up with a significantly lower total than you could have gotten if you'd made a more conservative second attempt. You will see many lifters fail their third attempts, but this is hardly surprising when you are pushing at the margins of your limits.

As you progress and compete more frequently, the weights you select will be determined by your competition goals on the day and these may vary between meets. For example, your main goal may be to hit a new total PB, just a PB on a certain lift, to hit a qualifying total (QT) for another competition, to test how a new program is working out, or maybe you just want to gain platform experience and get nine for nine (9/9) good lifts. Alternatively, you might be aiming for a place on the podium, in which case your attempt selection will depend on what the other competitors in your age and weight class are lifting. If considering this last option the website: https://www.openpowerlifting.org/ is a fabulous resource where you can check out the latest competition results and rankings of your competitors (and yourself after you have placed in a competition).

It is worth noting that QTs do vary between local, regional, and national competitions. For example, at the time of writing the IPF QTs for a Masters 2, -93 kg male were as follows: 435 kg (North West Championships), 470 kg (All England Championships), 495 kg (British Championships). Qualifying totals are reset each year based on championship performances and must be achieved at a sanctioned competition recognized by British Powerlifting. If a QT set in a particular category exceeds that of higher weight classes, the lifter may elect to lift in the higher weight class. Current national champions can defend their title without qualification but if they wish to compete at a different bodyweight they must make the QT for that bodyweight.

For your first few competitions you should aim for nine good lifts and if you can get these with 27 white lights (not a single referee failing one of your lifts) even better. Getting nine good lifts early on in your competition experience is a great confidence booster. It helps to develop a powerful 'can do' mindset, such that you will feel confident to complete all lifts for new PBs at subsequent competitions. Hitting 9/9 with relatively easy third attempts will also build your total quicker than hitting 6/9 with three failed third attempts!

The more you compete the better you will understand how you perform on the platform. People differ in how they respond to performing under pressure. For some it will have a beneficial impact and they will be able to hit new PBs above what they have previously hit in training. However, for others the impact will be detrimental and the pressure will serve to shave a small percentage off their training PBs.

Powerlifting competitions are really friendly events and it is easy to get talking with people and to make new friends. However, be warned that it is also very easy to let other people into your head and this can have all sorts of negative implications. In most cases this will be done without any malice, but in others a coach or lifter may deliberately try and mess with your head in order to give themselves or their lifter an advantage. You need to remember you have a plan already in place and you need to stick with it. It is your plan and nobody else's! Moreover, your plan has been honed over several months, so should be nice and sound!

Competition nutrition

Your competition food choices should start before the event, particularly if you are close to the upper bound of your weight limit. You need to make sure you weigh-in on target, but it is not that difficult to compromise this if you are cutting it close. As an example, those on a low carbohydrate diet (like myself) often consider upping their carbs a few days prior to the competition in order to replenish their muscle glycogen stores as a reserve energy source for the day. However, it must be remembered that for every gram of carbs stored as glycogen you will also store three to four grams of water! If you are closer to the lower bound limit of your weight class then carb loading in this way is not going to be a problem, but don't over do it. You might want to reduce your fat intake slightly to account for these additional carbs. Consuming carbs the day beforehand should make you feel more comfortable on the day.

On the day itself it is a good idea to try and avoid eating beforehand if the weigh-in is very early in the morning. The lighter you are on the scales the more competitive you will be in the event of an equal total with another lifter. However, if you do need to eat, then try and restrict this to small quantities of carb-rich foods. Likewise, if you have an afternoon weigh-in you will likely want to eat beforehand, but focus on foods that will help you through the event rather than hinder you. As soon as weigh-in has finished you can eat whatever you want and you will see lifters starting to stuff their faces with all sorts of different foods. The important thing here is to choose low fibre, carbohydrate-dense foods that you know you can easily digest. The aim is that this meal will provide you with slow-release energy for the duration of the competition, without being too voluminous or increasing the risk of gastrointestinal issues, e.g. bloating or more severe reactions in those who suffer with the likes of IBD or IBS. In short, this is not the time to start eating unfamiliar foods.

An important point to acknowledge is that competition day nutrition does not equate to typical healthy lifestyle nutrition. You may end up consuming two or three times your typical daily calorie intake, but don't worry about it. Your food choices on competition day need to provide you with a steady supply of energy throughout the duration of the event, but must not impede your performance. Your normal protein and fat intakes should be reduced in favour of carbohydrates, which are the preferred and most easily accessed source of energy. Aim for slow-release energy-rich foods, such as pasta, rice, low-fat cereals, etc. You can also include some quick-fix energy foods for consuming in small amounts as and when you feel you need them.

Good hydration is equally important and can include water, coffee, sports drinks, pre-workout drinks, etc. Sports drinks can be an effective way of consuming extra calories for those who may find eating on competition day problematic (for any number of reasons). Another option for easy extra calories are energy gels. Many of the aforementioned contain large quantities of caffeine, so take this into consideration if using various combinations of the above. If used wisely, caffeine will help you increase your energy and decrease your fatigue when it counts. The positive effects can be felt as soon as 15 minutes following consumption, with peak blood levels after about one hour and remaining at this level for several hours in most people. Hence, the effects of a coffee consumed after your bench press session should have kicked in by the time your deadlifts start.

It is a good idea to have a bottle of water with sports electrolytes added, but make sure you make up the solution to the correct concentration otherwise it defeats the objective. This should help prevent muscle cramps during the competition ... and I can state from personal experience that trying to walk off foot cramp between attempts in a relatively small flight of lifters is no fun at all.

If you lift in a drug-tested federation and choose to use pre-workout drinks make sure none of the ingredients are on the World Anti-Doping Agency (WADA) list of banned substances (https://www.wada-ama.org). This of course also goes for any medicines you routinely take, e.g. glucocorticoids which are prescribed for many common ailments. Therapeutic Use Exemption (TUE) certificates can be applied for and there is a new 2022 paper discussing this issue on the WADA website.

Make sure you have enough food and drink to keep you going throughout the competition – you will probably drink more than you expect. I always pack two flasks of coffee – I would rather have it and not drink it than really want one and not have any! I also keep an extra bottle of water in my car just in case. Likewise, it is never a good idea to run out of food and sometimes meets can run over time by several hours. Some venues have on-site caterers, some have shops in close proximity, others have nothing at all, especially if the competition falls on a Sunday as is often the case! Always be prepared for the latter regardless, then even if caterers cancel at the last minute (as happens often), or local shops are closed for one reason or another, you will still be OK. Of course, if you have any food allergies make sure you bring appropriate nutrition with you because it is unlikely you will be able to find any speciality caterers on site.

Lastly, as a word of warning, avoid too much sugary food and fizzy drinks, especially if these are not something you normally consume. Eating too much refined sugar, especially in the absence of protein, fibre, fats, etc. can result in a rapid 'sugar crash'. When the body has more sugar than usual, it rapidly produces insulin in an attempt to keep the levels consistent, which causes blood glucose to decrease and results in a sudden drop in energy levels, ability to concentrate and various other symptoms that will not help you lift heavy iron! As for fizzy drinks, the internet is replete with film footage of lifters projectile vomiting all over the centre referee, whilst trying to grind out a heavy deadlift. Whilst this can occur for a number of different reasons, at least in some cases this is probably mainly due to downing a full can of fizzy energy drink shortly before the attempt. Do not be this person ... you will likely never live it down!

The author failing a 200 kg deadlift attempt (for a new competition PB) at the All England Championships, 2022 – this is as far as it went. Image credit WLM.

Failing lifts

There are a number of reasons why you might fail each of the lifts, ranging from the load being too heavy to not following the commands correctly or any number of minor technical infringements and some of these were discussed earlier. Other rules include, if using wrist wraps, the thumb loop must NOT be placed around the thumb; if wearing knee sleeves for deadlifts, then the bottom of these must not be touching the top of the socks. It is important to familiarize yourself with the 'rule book' (which should be available on your division website page) in order to minimize the likelihood of technical mishaps. There is nothing worse than grinding out a new PB on a lift only to start racking it before the 'rack' command and have the lift disqualified as a result.

We all fail lifts. It is just part of the process, especially when we are pushing at the boundaries of our physical capabilities. Hence, it is not uncommon to see a lifter fail their third attempt, or even their second. What should not happen though is for a lifter to fail their first attempt. This is basically down to either bad planning with regard to weight selection or lack of familiarity with the rules. Your first attempt should be an easy lift in order to get yourself on the score sheet and secure a place and final total in the competition. Remember, if you fail all three attempts of any of the lifts you 'bomb out' and cannot place or secure a total. Lifters can change their opening attempt up until shortly before the start of the flight. Don't wait until it's too late. The table crew should (but don't always) announce when the cut-off time is approaching and once it has passed you will not be able to change your opener. The general rule of thumb is that the table staff must be notified at least three minutes before the beginning of your flight or three lifters before the end of the flight preceding yours. Be sensible about this and do not be afraid to utilize this option (I have done it several times). If you are warming up and the bar feels too heavy or you are struggling, drop the weight on your opener.

Three points to remember if you do fail a lift. First, you are quite entitled to quickly ask the referee on your way off the platform why you failed the lift. Indeed, this is the best time to do it because they will be unlikely to remember if you ask them after the flight has finished. Second, fail the lift with good grace, sportsmanship and decorum. Do not start throwing a tantrum and do not swear on the platform. Swearing on the platform is against the rules. You may get a warning the first time, but repeat swearing can lead to disqualification. Third, if you feel you are about to fail a squat due to it being too heavy NEVER, EVER throw the bar! You are likely

Opposite page: I never notice the spotters during my lifts, as I am so focused on the lift itself. However, they do a remarkable job of keeping the lifters safe on the platform and I am very grateful for their presence. Make sure you also look after them by taking as much weight of the bar as you can whilst they help you re-rack a failed lift attempt. All England Championships, 2022. Image credit WLM.

to injure yourself and your spotters. There will be at least three spotters supporting you and if you start to fail the lift they will quickly step in to help you out. Their job is to help you re-rack the bar, but you will still be expected to bear most of the weight and walk it back into the rack.

From a personal perspective, I have failed all three lifts for various reasons. I have failed squats on not quite reaching depth, bench press on pressing before the 'press' command and also due to the weight being too heavy, deadlifts due to the weight being too heavy ... but I have never bombed out of a competition due to failing all my attempts at a single lift as a result of setting my opener too high ... yet. My biggest fail to date was having to re-rack my opening squat even before beginning the lift due to the resurgence of a recent lower back injury. I knew immediately that it was bad enough for me to withdraw from the competition. I re-racked the bar without fuss and left the platform so the bar could be prepared for the next lifter ... the show must go on!

It is important to appreciate that competition lifting is very different to gym training. The amount of fatigue that accumulates throughout a three-lift competition is considerable, so that by the time you get around to your final bench and deadlifts, it can become impossible to complete lifts with weights that move relatively easily in the gym.

A final point to consider is training for responding to the lift commands well in advance of the event. You may be confident that you know the order of commands for the different lifts, but when you step on the platform at competition, your focus on completing a heavy lift can sometimes lead you to completely forget to pause at the end of the lift and start to rack the bar before the 'rack' command has been given. In part, this is a survival strategy whereby when under extreme pressure, higher-order cognitive (brain) functions (including remembering that you need to wait for the referee commands) get shut down or bypassed in order that a faster, but more primitive neural network takes over (the so-called fight, flight or freeze response). This can happen on the platform and may be due to trying to shift an extremely heavy load that is threatening to crush you, or it may be something as simple as performing in front of a referee or audience. Regardless, the 'brain freeze' that can result is easily enough to make you forget to wait for the rack command. Sometimes you will hear coaches shouting 'wait' or some similar cue to their lifters once they have locked-out at the end of a lift.

The author being helped by Darren Stafford at his first sanctioned (Novice) competition, 2018. Image credit LD.

When you fail a lift, and it will happen at some point, you have two choices: 1. You can dwell on it and let the frustration this causes affect the rest of your competition performance. 2. You can focus on managing your emotions, quickly forget that the fail ever happened and concentrate on successfully completing your next lift. Your competition game plan should be sufficiently flexible and organized that for every lift you make, you already have your next attempt planned, both in the event of failure or successful completion of the lift. The same holds true if you are unfortunate enough to bomb out of a competition. Do not dwell on it, such things happen, get over it and get on with training for your next event. Learn from the experience and do not make the same mistake again.

As a general rule, it is not a good idea to increase weight on your second attempt if you received a no lift on your opener, even if the fail was based on a minor technical detail. Whatever the reason for the fail, you made a mistake, so do not compound the problem by making another. Keep the same weight for your second attempt and get yourself on the scoreboard. Increasing weight after a failed opener increases the risk of failing all three lifts and bombing out of the competition. It does happen!

Should you use a handler/coach or manage yourself?

Many competitors arrive with their coach (if they have one) or with a fellow lifter who may not be lifting that day, but who has experience of competitions and who can act as a 'handler'. The handler has several functions at a meet, probably the most important of which is making sure that the lifter is in the right place at the right time, e.g. for weigh-in, rack hight measurements, and of course that they are ready to step on the platform when it is there turn to do so! From the time at which "The bar is loaded" alert is given, the lifter has just one minute to get on the platform and start the lift and it is not unusual to see somebody dashing onto the platform with a few seconds to spare ... just try to make sure it isn't you. Your handler can also make sure you are fully ready to lift before you approach the platform, for example, that your back is chalked (should you wish to do so), wrist wraps are properly secured and that you are wearing your belt (it is not unheard of for a lifter to approach the bar for a heavy deadlift only to realize they have forgotten their belt ... and for them to dash back off again in order to retrieve it!). Clearly, this is not the best way to set up for a new deadlift PB!

The handler is also there to help the lifter warm-up, not too early and not too late and to make sure they don't burn themselves out during the warm-up by doing too much volume or too many heavy reps. They should also load the plates for the warm-ups in order to minimize fatigue in the lifter. They are there to encourage the lifter and help motivate them, when they may have conflicting emotions or be nervous, especially if it is their first competition.

They can also help the lifter decide on their next lift attempt numbers and give this information to the table staff, whilst the lifter is recovering from their previous attempt (you have just one minute to provide the next attempt information following the previous lift, otherwise a standard increment of just 2.5 kg will be added automatically). Ideally, the handler should be familiar with the abilities of the lifter, including their current PBs, comp total PB and should keep an eye on any close competitors in order to determine any subsequent attempts that may be required to secure their lifter a win.

There is no obligation to have a coach or handler and many lifters train alone and turn up for competitions by themselves. Once you have done a few meets it is easy enough to make sure you are doing the right things in the right place at the right time. Personally, I look after myself when it comes to both training and competitions, although at my first sanctioned competition Darren Stafford (WolfpackStrength, Stalybridge) took it upon himself to look after me throughout the event (despite having other lifters of his own) and I was very grateful for his assistance at the time.

After the competition

Before leaving the venue, it is always polite to thank the organizers, platform crew and the referees who usually give up their time on a volunteer basis in order to make the competitions a success. Double check that you have all your kit and make sure you have not left any mess behind for anybody else to clear up.

Critically appraise your performance in terms of whether or not you managed to fulfil your competition goals and, if not, what happened to prevent this and how could you overcome any similar hurdles next time. Make sure you take several days to a week off from training in order to recover from the meet. Although you may not feel exhausted your body will soon let you know it needs a rest if you do not heed this advice.

A review and critical appraisal of my first sanctioned competition

My formal debut as a competitive powerlifter was at a novice competition in Liverpool in January 2018, just 10 weeks before my 50th birthday. It represented a significant milestone in my powerlifting journey and was what the previous six months of training and nutritional discipline had been about. My game plan all along had been to hit a qualifying total for the Masters 2 (-83kg) British Championships and I exceeded this by 10kg, though it did not all go as planned.

I did not feel as nervous as I expected, but then again I was 'in the zone'. I had my focus and I had what I considered a realistic (based on my training experience) game plan. In addition, I had a very experienced guy in my corner who fired me up, coached me through my lift attempts and ran my numbers for me. I was very grateful to Darren Stafford for this … he saw I was on my own, so offered to help me out and looked after me as if I was one of his own competitors. This took a

lot of pressure off me and allowed me to focus on the lifts and he also taught me some very useful competition day tips! At the outset, my plan was to do it all by myself because that is what I am used to and how I normally operate. However, in retrospect I was very happy to have Darren on my side and would strongly recommend that any lifter have a good coach with them, especially for their first competition.

My original plan was to hit the Qualifying Total on each of my second lift attempts, which were planned as follows: Squat: 120 kg, 130 kg, 135 kg; Bench: 95 kg, 105 kg, 110 kg; Deadlift: 150 kg, 160 kg, 170 kg ... but not everything went to plan:

Squat: The opener of the first lift is the most important lift of your first competition as a successful attempt boosts the confidence significantly. I felt fine walking on to the platform and was confident with the weight, but did have a couple of surprises. I was used to being able to rotate the bar when I set up, but was unable to do this on the platform set-up. Nonetheless, I unracked the bar and stepped back to await the 'squat' command ... which did not come as I had expected. The problem was that I had not locked my knees out properly and the referee was waiting for me to do so. After a while she instructed me to do this (it being a novice competition) and

The author squatting 135 kg as his third attempt at his first sanctioned (Novice) competition, Liverpool, 2018. Image credit LD.

127

The author bench pressing 95 kg as an opener at his first sanctioned (Novice) competition, Liverpool, 2018. Image credit LD.

then gave the squat command. The upshot of this is that I was standing around with a weighted bar on my back for longer than I had anticipated and the unforeseen set-up issue had a minor impact on my mindset for my opener as I was musing over it as I performed the rep. Of course, this was entirely my own fault as it was a set-up issue I was unaware of. I did not know the rules sufficiently well. I completed the opener successfully and encountered no similar problems in the following two attempts. Opener of 120 kg, followed by 130 kg and 135 kg. Prior to the competition I was a little concerned at making depth for the heavier reps and getting the bar back up again, as I had struggled a little with this during training. However, my second and third attempts felt reasonably easy and I reckon I could have gone a bit heavier.

Bench press: I felt confident and strong. No problem with the opener of 95 kg, but I could not quite get the second attempt of 105 kg past the sticking point. I tried the same weight for my third attempt and had the same problem. I'd had a similar problem with this once during training, though I had usually been able to hit it. Regardless, I was still in the game, having made a good first lift, but I needed to revise my planned deadlift attempts if I still wanted to make a qualifying total on the sum of my second attempts. I really did not want to leave that total in the fate of my final lift of the day!

Deadlift: I maintained my planned 150 kg opener, which went up easily, despite me waiting for a command to lift from the referee (there is no command to initiate the deadlift, beyond the 'bar is loaded' statement). Another example of not knowing the rules, but that is, in part, what novice competitions are about ... make mistakes and learn from them! I then went for 165 kg to hit the qualifying total and that too felt easy, so I put in for 175 kg for the final attempt. This represented a new PB lift at my current bodyweight and the last time I tried it in the gym it did not get off the floor. Again, it flew up and I reckon I could have gone heavier.

The author deadlifting 175 kg as a third attempt at his first sanctioned (Novice) competition, Liverpool, 2018. Image credit LD.

Some final reflections: Basically, some of the lifts I expected to be difficult (and potentially fail) felt quite easy, i.e. the heavier squats and heaviest deadlift, whereas others that I expected to feel relatively easy (the second bench attempt), I failed … twice! It just goes to show how competition day is different from a regular gym training day.

My final total was 405 kg. In my category of -83 kg I hit the National Qualifying Total. Out of the total of 52 lifters, 15 people hit British Qualifying Totals and eight hit the slightly lower English Qualifying Totals. Regardless, everybody qualified as a competitive powerlifter and that is something to be proud of and although you compete alongside and against others, the main competition is yourself (we all got new competition PBs!). It is about what *you* can do and next time will be about doing it better than you did the last time. Following the competition I did a deload week in the gym, then got back to training for the next comp.

I had a good sleep and woke up early on competition day. Even after a small but very strong coffee (300ml mug, I normally have 1000ml!) I still had around 1.5 kg of bodyweight to play with ... but considered it 0.5 kg to err on the safe side and account for my home scales being inaccurate! Hence, I was able to have a snack before weigh in at 12.30 just to raise my blood sugar and stop me feeling really crappy. In order to compete in the -83kg weight class, I had been on a very gradual weight cut since July, so for a full six-months and had been increasing my strength at the same time. On the day I weighted in at 81.3kg. In terms of body fat % I look and felt like I was in the best shape of my life ... back in a 32" waist, down from 46-48" just a few years earlier. However, maintaining this low body fat in order to fit into the -83kg category had required a lot of discipline and was starting to grate on me (just a little bit) towards the end stages. I looked forward to after the weigh in when I no longer needed to worry about this for a while.

On competition day I ate my standard breakfast and made sure I had sufficient food and drink for the day. I chose to travel to the venue by train as it was only supposed to take 55 minutes from Manchester. However, there was a points problem on the line and the journey ended up taking 2.5 hours! Fortunately, I had set off much earlier than I needed to because I wanted to watch a friend in the morning session. I was given a real run-around by the train service and was sent to several different stations in order to make connections and given conflicting information. Under normal circumstances I am quite certain I would have been very miffed by this. I did not want to miss this comp, especially as I had to pull out of a previous one due to injury. However, I was remarkably calm about it. Clearly, I was 'in the zone', and I was not about to let external factors affect that ... I had the 'it is what it is' mentality and given there was nothing I could do to change the situation, it did not warrant me stressing over it (at the potential expense of my competition performance later on). I did casually mull over the potential plan B of getting a taxi to the venue if things looked like they were getting really bad, but fortunately it did not come to this. I made it just in time for weigh-in.

I thoroughly enjoyed the day and achieved the goal I set out to. The competition ran smoothly, the atmosphere was great and everybody seemed really friendly. It was a great introduction to formal powerlifting.

Summary of rookie mistakes to avoid at your first competition

- Arriving late for weigh-in and/or not making weight on the day.
- Forgetting certain items of kit or your federation membership card. It is a good idea to store all your competition kit together in a special place, so you know exactly where it all is. You may end up having 12 months between competitions and it is very easy to forget where you have put things if you store it all separately.
- Having non-approved items of kit.
- Doing it by yourself. Bring an experienced friend or coach to help with the competition logistics.
- Cutting body weight to make a weight class. You can do this for later competitions if need be in order to gain competitive advantage, but it is not a good idea for your first competition.
- Running out of food and drink. Competitions often run on for longer than anticipated and it is always better to have too much than too little. Don't rely on there being anywhere local to purchase any, as you may end up disappointed and hungry.
- Bringing the wrong kind of food and drinks. Avoid fizzy drinks (although you will see many people swigging down cans of fizzy energy drinks) and foods that are going to sit heavy in your stomach. Aim for slow release energy foods and quick fix energy snacks, but avoid overdosing on sugar.
- Setting your openers too high and/or not having a flexible plan for subsequent attempts. Competition lifting is not the same as gym/training lifting. Do not expect an 'adrenaline factor' of participating to help lift greater weights.
- Forgetting (or missing the one minute deadline) to submit your next attempt to the table staff following your previous lift.
- Not knowing (and/or not waiting for) the referees commands for the lifts or other basic competition rules.
- Missing (or almost missing) an attempt because you did not keep a close eye on the running order.
- Losing sight of the fact that this should be a fun event. Whatever you walk away with will be a new competition PB.

What else could possibly go wrong?

As you start working with heavier weights in your competition peaking phase the risk of injury increases as a result of overload stress. It is imperative that you take great care to focus on your technique for each and every rep and if you have a training plan make sure you stick to it. I have learnt both these lessons the hard way. On more than one occasion I have pulled my back doing heavy deadlifts just a few weeks out from competition, which meant I had to compete as a bench-only lifter, which is far from ideal. I suspect this was partly due to my competition belt being far inferior to my training belt, so when I switched over getting close to the competition I was not getting the same degree of support. I now have a top quality competition belt, so this is no longer a problem.

Thursday, November 7, 2019 started off just like any normal weekday. I was up at around 4:30 am and left the house before the crack of dawn to get to the gym for opening time at 6:00 am. It was just over four weeks before my next full-power competition and I was making good progress and looking set to hit new competition personal bests on all three lifts. It was squat day and I had my work plan in place: warm-ups, followed by 120 kg, 130 kg, 140 kg, 145 kg, 150 kg, 155 kg, 160 kg, 165 kg, followed by some back-off sets. As I worked up to 140 kg, the bar was flying up and I was feeling strong, so decided to skip the 145 kg and go straight to 150 kg. This should not have been a problem given that I hit a good 160 kg lift the week previously.

However, on the day, something went wrong and I just lost the groove of the lift and was unable to lift the bar all the way back up again. I dropped myself to the floor 'safe' in the knowledge that the rack I was squatting in would catch the bar, which it did. This was only the second time I had needed to do this. Unfortunately, the tip of the ring finger of my right hand managed to get crushed between the bar and the rack. I don't recall exactly what happened next or what the immediate thought was that went through my head, but I needed to twist myself in a rather awkward position to free my finger from beneath the knurling of the bar, which no doubt compounded the damage somewhat.

I knew I had done something bad, but did not know how bad, and quickly grabbed the end of my finger in my good hand in order to prevent any possibility of blood spraying all over the place. I made my way quickly to the changing room and washed the wound off and dried the area with some paper tissue. It was immediately evident that a trip to the hospital would be required. I fetched some electrical tape from my car and then covered the wound up with more tissue paper after taking some photographs, so I could show the hospital staff the damage without having to remove my makeshift dressing.

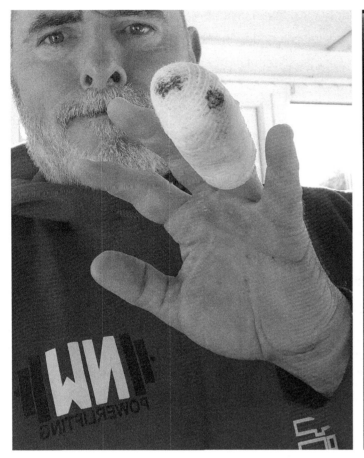
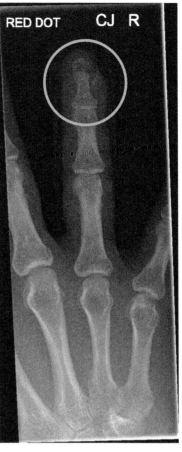

The result of a 150 kg squat fail finger crush injury just four weeks before a competition, November, 2019.

After several hours, I eventually had the wound irrigated and bandaged up and received a tetanus prophylaxis jab, was given a dose of intravenous antibiotics and provided with a 5-day course of oral antibiotics before being sent for x-rays, which clearly showed gross soft tissue swelling, a comminuted burst type fracture affecting the tuft of the distal phalanx and a displaced bone fragment seen at the medial aspect of the distal phalanx.

It was explained to me that I would need an operation in a few days to clean up the wound, but nothing was certain at this stage. The worst-case scenario was amputation of the finger-tip … it was going to be a waiting game. Finally, I was sent home to await a formal appointment for surgery. I had a large bandage over the finger, which prevented me from doing pretty much anything with it.

My surgery for finger repair and debridement (removal of dead tissue/foreign objects) was confirmed for the following Tuesday (12 November, less than three weeks out from competition day) and my wound kept gradually weeping blood up until that point. As they were preparing me for theatre, I was asked my bodyweight as I was lying on the trolley. I do remember the anaesthetist not believing me when I told her it was 100kg and she suggested I was probably around 90kg. I assured her that I wasn't and that I weighed myself every day in the gym! They had marked my arm and finger with arrows, so I was pretty confident I was going to come out with a fixed digit rather than a new kidney.

I had opted for sedation rather than a general anaesthetic, but for all intents and purposes it may as well have been the latter, as I do not recall a thing. I left hospital with a bandage of similar size to the one I had entered with, albeit much cleaner and by the time I went to bed there was still no discomfort, but the analgesics gradually wore off and I awoke at about 1:00 am with my finger throbbing. When I awoke the following morning my finger felt fine, but I was surprised at the pains and marks around my right hand and chest. They must have strapped me down with something that I can only imagine resembled something from a Medieval torture chamber. I had not experienced any significant pain at all, even when the accident happened or following it and I was not sure whether this was a good sign or not. There was still a lack of clarity regarding whether the finger tip would need amputation or not, so it was very much a waiting game to see how the wound repaired.

The first time I got to see the wound again was when the District Nurse changed the dressing a few days after the operation. I was very surprised at how good it looked, though there was still a considerable degree or swelling and redness. Fortunately, there was no sign of any leakage from the wound and this remained the case when it was checked again by a Consultant in Trauma and Orthopaedics one week later (19 November).

The stitches were removed the following week (26 November) and the Consultant deemed the finger tip to be viable, so at last I had positive confirmation that there would be no need to amputate it. I asked the Consultant about getting back to the gym and powerlifting and the fact that I had a competition place booked in just under two weeks. Not surprisingly, he told me it was not a good idea and that there was no way I should consider competing. Of course, I agreed, especially since not being able to train since the accident more than two weeks previously.

I left with a much-reduced finger bandage, which permitted slightly more flexibility of my finger, so I decided to get back in the gym and see what I could do with regards to my heavy lifts. I had already been back in the gym since Wednesday, 20 November, but had just been doing some light pushing work and no pulling. It wasn't until Friday, 29 November, and after the stitches had been removed, that I decided to test my heavy lifts and to my amazement I was able to complete all three lifts as follows: Squat 135 kg, Bench Press 110 kg, Deadlift 170 kg, even without being able to grip the bar fully with my right hand. I returned again on Sunday for lifts of 140, 112.5 and 175 kg respectively. My bench and deadlifts were down and would remain so for a while, as a result of the grip issue. However, there was just an ever so slight chance that I may be able to work my squat up in time to hit a new Comp PB at the competition the following weekend.

I knew it was ill advised to compete so soon after the injury and everybody I spoke to in the gym confirmed this, but something kept stopping me from emailing my withdrawal to the event organizer, even though I had every intention of sending it. And so it was, that the following weekend I took to the platform at the Fighting Fit Christmas Spectacular 2019 (8 December), with the following results: Squat 140 kg, 147.5 kg, ~~152.5~~ kg; Bench Press 105 kg, 110 kg, 112.5 kg; Deadlift 165 kg, 175 kg, ~~177.5~~ kg, for a total of 435kg. I had a 2:1 fail for depth on my final squat, which having been viewed by other coaches would have been a good lift (and a new PB) on a different day. When I watched the movie clip, it was very close indeed, though I must admit it did not feel quite deep enough at the time, so I was not surprised by the two red lights. My final bench press was down on my previous competition, but was still nonetheless a British Qualifying Total, so I couldn't really complain about that either. Overall, I was down only 22.5kg from the NW Masters competition four months earlier and following the Christmas competition I trained steadily and managed to hit a new PB of 122.5 kg at the British Bench Press Championships on 23 February 2020, before the Corona virus epidemic kicked in and threw a spanner in the works once again.

Six months later my finger had just about fully healed and the nail was almost fully grown back. Having watched various other squat fail movie clips online, I have seen something very similar almost happen to others and I doubt none of those involved realized how close they came to having a nasty injury. Hence, it may be that this is not such an uncommon injury, though it was one that I was totally unaware of. Please don't let it happen to you. The moral of the story: When you have a plan, stick to it … it was designed that way for good reason! It is also a very good idea to practice failing with light weights, so that in the event you fail with a heavy load and don't have a spotter helping out, you will be better able to deal with it safely.

How many competitions should you do?

Once you have completed your first competition it is highly likely that you will start to think about when you can do another! Between local divisional events and larger national competitions (assuming you have hit the appropriate Qualifying Totals) there should be ample opportunity to compete numerous times each year. Since starting, I have competed three or four times per year, except for 2020 when competitions were cancelled due to lockdown. So long as you can keep making progress each time you compete then you are not doing too many. Try and make sure there are at least 12–16 weeks between competitions in order to facilitate recovery and new strength gains.

As you progress with your lifting it is probably a good idea to set the number of competitions to around three. Just doing a single competition annually is not really sufficient to give you enough platform time to develop your confidence, focus and competitive edge, whereas doing too many will not allow you to have a rest period and/or focus more on developing your strength in the gym. If you wish to compete in a 'Championships' competition (internationally, nationally or regionally) then a qualifying total will most likely need to be achieved at an earlier event within the preceding 12 months, so that will require a minimum of two competitions. Throw in an additional local divisional or charity event and that should be sufficient for the year. Obviously, there are no hard and fast rules in this regard.

My competition history is shown in the table below (the dip in performance in December 2019 was due to a finger crush injury and the dip in performance at the 2021 NW Masters was due to the COVID lockdown – the aim here was just to get back on the platform, take it easy and secure the second place as I had no chance of placing first). The significant bodyweight increase in 2019/2020 into the -105 kg class was due to a dietary change in order to help manage ulcerative colitis (UC), with which I was diagnosed in November 2018. This worked for a while until I had two courses of antibiotics for my finger crush injury, which sent me back into a minor flare, which persisted for quite some time. I subsequently transitioned to a carnivore-type diet in March 2021, again in an attempt to manage my UC and the consequence of this was that it stripped my body fat percentage right down and I ended up back in the -93 kg class.

Table showing competition data for the author (shaded cells = new PBs, * = new bodyweight PB; † = had to rerack opening squat and withdraw from competition due to recurrence of lower back injury)

Competition	Date	Age	Class	Weight	Squat	Bench	Deadlift	Total
NW Novice 2018	13/1/18	49	-83	81.3kg	135	95	175	405
NW Bench 2018	3/6/18	50	-83	81.4	–	102.5	–	–
NW Championships	7/7/18	50	-93	85.2	–	115	–	–
NW Masters 2019	18/8/19	51	-105	99.2	150	120	187.5	457.5
NW Xmas Spectacular	7/12/19	51	-105	100	147.5	112.5	175	435
British Bench Champs	23/2/20	51	-105	100.4	–	122.5	–	–
British Bench Champs	7/8/21	53	-93	86.5	–	105	–	–
NW Masters 2021	21/8/21	53	-93	85.9	120	107.5	172.5	400
NW Bench 2021	21/8/21	53	-93	85.9	–	107.5	–	–
NW Xmas Spectacular	5/12/21	53	-93	88.7	152.5	115	192.5	460
NW Winter Open	12/2/22	53	-93	91.6	–	122.5*	–	–
All Englands Champs	29/5/22	54	-93	89.4	155	122.5*	195	472.5
NW Masters 2022	20/8/22	54	-93	91.1	157.5	120	205	482.5
NW Champs 2022	26/11/22	54	-93	90.5	–†	–	–	–

Weight class selection – some considerations

As a new (but not so young), independent lifter just starting out and considering entering a competition, an important question I asked myself was: *Which weight class would be optimum for me?* Should I enter at my current weight, should I bulk up to the next class, or should I cut down to the class below? As already mentioned, it is ill advised to cut weight before your first competition, but on the other hand there are folks who consistently train at the bottom of the weight class above and then cut aggressively pre-comp to sit competitively at the top end of their competition weight class. This can often be a close call and there is the risk of not making your weight class at all, which would exclude you from placing at the competition. This option is usually chosen by those who tend to take the sport a little more seriously. Certainly it is not a good idea to cut weight for your first competition even if you are close to the lower-bound limit of your current weight class.

Sometimes there may be a competitive advantage to switching your weight class due to the number of active lifters in a particular class and this is more evident the further you move up the Masters age class categories. I have now competed in three different weight classes (-83 kg, -93 kg, -105 kg) in 14 sanctioned competitions, one NWPL club competition and a couple of charity events. Due to the odd back tweak here and there my squats and deadlifts had not increased over time as much as they could have done. Consequently, assessing these data do not add much to the weight class debate so will be ignored and I will focus on my bench press results, which have not been affected by these particular injuries. However, various other life events have impacted on my bench as will be discussed.

Table showing competition bench press data for the author at different weight classes (shaded cells = new sanctioned PBs, * = new bodyweight PB)

Competition	Date	Age	Class	Weight	Lift 1	Lift 2	Lift 3
NW Novice 2018	13/1/18	49	-83	81.3kg	95	105	105
Fighting Fit Club Comp	18/2/18	49	-83	83	100	105	110
NW Bench Champs 2018	3/6/18	50	-83	81.4	95	100	102.5
NW Championships 2018	7/7/18	50	-93	85.2	105	110	115
NW Masters Champs 2019	18/8/19	51	-105	99.2	117.5	120	122.5
NW Xmas Spectacular 2019	7/12/19	51	-105	100	105	110	112.5
British Bench Champs 2020	23/2/20	51	-105	100.4	115	120*	122.5
British Bench Champs 2021	7/8/21	53	-93	86.5	105	110	110
NW Masters Champs 2021	21/8/21	53	-93	85.9	105	107.5	110
NW Bench Champs 2021	21/8/21	53	-93	85.9	105	107.5	110
NW Xmas Spectacular	5/12/21	53	-93	88.7	115	120	120
NW Winter Open 2022	12/2/22	53	-93	91.6	120	122.5*	125
All Englands Champs 2022	29/5/22	54	-93	89.4	122.5*	125	125
NW Masters Champs 2022	20/8/22	54	-93	91.1	115	120	125

I started training powerlifting in the -93 kg class, but did not compete formally until I had cut down to the -83 kg class. Newbie gains were made relatively easily over my first two comps, but by the time I weighed in at my third competition at 81.4 kg my body fat was very low indeed. I looked totally ripped and at 50 years-old had a six-pack that put most youngsters to shame. However, I soon realized that this was not sustainable, especially if I wanted to increase my strength significantly. At the North West Bench Championships my top lift was a mere 102.5 kg, which I was very disappointed with, as my training lifts at just a few kg bodyweight heavier had been around 115 kg, and I was hoping to open at 110 kg on the day!

Indeed, I was so miffed with this result that I immediately registered for the North West Championships which was due to happen approximately four weeks later, but I entered in the -93 kg class and decided I was not going to worry about my weight for that one and started eating my way up. I felt much better and managed 115 kg for a new comp PB on the day and decided I would remain in the -93 kg class and this would still work aesthetically.

In October 2018 I became unwell and in December of that year was diagnosed with ulcerative colitis. I was prescribed, amongst other things, corticosteroids, a side-effect of which is that you want to eat EVERYTHING! I had recently seen a friend go

The author
benching at
the North West
Bench Press
Championships,
2018.

from a very strong and well-built 90+ kg, waste away to 40+ kg and almost die as a
result of IBD, so I decided that if I was going to experience anything similar then I
wanted sufficient body reserves to help me through, which my current low body fat
was not likely to provide. I also changed my diet completely in an attempt to help
manage the condition and so it was that I happily and intentionally headed up to the
-105 kg class. Fortunately, my IBD went into remission and my first competition at
this weight (North West Masters) saw me hit a 120 kg bench press, representing a 5
kg increase on my comp PB and I was looking forwards to extending this further at
the North West Christmas Spectacular a few months later.

However, life struck again four weeks before the comp, this time in the form of a
very nasty finger crush injury (discussed earlier), which resulted in a real bloody
mess of ripped flesh and shattered bone and there was talk of having to amputate

The author bench pressing at the British Bench Press Championships, 2021, where he placed 2nd in the -93 kg, M2 class. Image credit WLM.

the tip, though fortunately this was not necessary. I was unable to do any lifting at the gym for two weeks and only moderate lifting for a week or so after that.

I still managed to compete but my weights were way down, at just 112.5 kg for my third attempt. Undeterred, I signed up for the British Bench Press Championships 2020, despite experiencing a resurgence of my IBD symptoms due to the antibiotic treatment received for my finger injury! I opened at 115 kg and walked away with a new comp PB of 122.5 kg and second place in my M2 weight category; I had planned for 125 or 127.5, but don't think I would have hit them on the day, though I certainly expected to at my next competition, but then COVID lockdowns kicked in, resulting in closed gyms and no comps.

At the end of March 2021 I embarked on the carnivore diet in an attempt to resolve my IBD symptoms and on the whole it seemed to work reasonably quickly. It also resulted in the rapid loss of excess body fat, taking me back down to the -93kg class again. After an 18-month COVID-induced competition hiatus I was easing myself back into competing, hitting new bodyweight bench press PBs from December 2021 onwards.

So, what conclusions can we take away from this? Certainly, there is a correlation between bodyweight and amount of weight lifted, and this was particularly evident at the British Bench Press Championships 2020. However, this is never going to be a nice linear or smooth curve due to life events and there are plenty of very light lifters shifting very heavy loads also. If you are just starting off in powerlifting experiment a little during the early years to see what suits you best. However, if you flip between weight classes too much you may find that you become ineligible for a later competition that might require a different Qualifying Total at your new bodyweight. If you want to compete by cutting weight aggressively prior to comp day take advice from an experienced coach with a good track record of success in employing this technique.

The author with medal and trophy at the British Bench Press Championships, 2020, having placed 2nd in the -105 kg, M2 class. Image credit WLM.

141

Selecting a Gym and Training Equipment

It should come as no surprise that not all gyms are created equal and this is especially true with regards to training for powerlifting! The worst thing you could probably do is head down to your nearest gym and sign yourself up to a 12-month contract. This is because, unless you are very lucky, the closest gym to you will probably not be the best local gym to fulfil all your training needs. In addition, it needs to be somewhere you are going to be happy because you will be spending a considerable amount of time there! Going to the gym should not seem like a chore. You need to find a place that you cannot wait to get in to and get down to business. You will need to do some research and visit as many gyms as necessary until you find the one that is right for you.

What should you be looking for in your gym?

The main training elements of your program will revolve around three basic exercises: squat, bench press and deadlift, all of which involve the use of a barbell and free weight plates. As the name suggests, the bench press will involve the use of a bench, the squat will require a squat rack or similar. For example, some gyms have functional training rigs with adjustable barbell hooks, which can be positioned high for doing squats or low in order to do the bench press. Finally, you will need somewhere to deadlift. Some gyms have specialized platforms designed for this purpose, whereas others do not allow deadlifting at all because the noise can disturb other users of the facility ... stay well clear of these gyms!

Most new gyms have rows upon rows of shiny cardio equipment, such as treadmills, exercise bikes, rowing machines, stepper machines and cross trainers. If you are lucky there may be a single squat rack and possibly a few benches. This is not the gym for you! You need to be able to walk into your gym and get straight on with your training, rather than having to hang around waiting for someone else to finish their routine in order to free up the piece of equipment that you need. Some of the newer gyms in larger commercial chains now include a large number of substantial squat racks with associated deadlift platforms. This is a good trend!

Checklist of equipment to look for in the gym

Mandatory

- Power racks and/or squat racks (or functional training rigs with adjustable hooks)
- Fixed bench (with uprights) for the bench press
- Movable benches (that can be moved into squat racks or rigs) for bench pressing
- Barbells (preferably quite a few)
- A good number and range of weight plates (even better if they are competition spec plates)

Preferred

- A good range of dumbbells (from light to heavy, e.g. 50 kg)
- Calibrated, competition spec kit, including plates, racks and benches
- Sauna (it is always nice to relax after the odd heavy workout)
- On-site certified strength and conditioning (or even better, powerlifting) coach

Optional

- Anything else, such as the cardio equipment and all the other weight-training machines you are likely to find in most gyms these days.

In addition to the above, the gym you choose must permit the use of traditional weightlifting/gymnastics chalk. Many gyms do not allow the use of liquid chalk because it can make a right mess of the barbells by clogging up in the knurling and that is fair enough. However, if the gym you are considering joining does not allow the use of conventional chalk (usually because the staff consider it to be too messy, which it doesn't need to be) then it is not the right gym for you! Move along to the next one.

You should be able to get a good feel for the ambience of a particular gym when you visit and take a look around. Unless you can find a gym that caters specifically for powerlifters (which is what you will be doing) then what you should be looking for is a reasonably diverse clientele who seem to be getting on with things, but at the same time interacting with each other in a pleasant way (it is not all about hard work all the time). A good mixture of men and women covering a broad age range is also a good sign.

Clearly, it is best to do your gym research at the same time of day that you intend to train. You will probably find that the smaller, private gyms have a more pleasant and less formal feel to them than the larger commercial gym chains, in addition to having a better range of equipment more suited to your specific training needs (though this is not always the case). The former tend to attract people that aim to get things done and make serious progress, whereas the latter are largely set up to cater for the (usually temporary) post-Christmas influx and this also tends to be reflected in the quality and relevant knowledge of the gym staff.

You can also search for suitable gyms online. There are plenty of good powerlifting groups on most social media platforms and it is common for people visiting unfamiliar regions (maybe for holiday or work purposes) to ask if there are any powerlifting friendly gyms in the area. Members of the group always provide valuable assistance and information in this regard.

Gym etiquette

Once you have found the right gym make sure you follow these simple rules so that you do not upset other people that use the facilities:

Do: have good hygiene, wear appropriate clothes, keep a respectful distance, allow others to work in where reasonable, be courteous and respectful of others, re-rack weights, treat the equipment with respect, clean up any mess you make (including wiping sweat off machines, benches, etc.), help people if they are clearly having difficulty, leave your ego at the door.

Don't: hog equipment (especially if all you are doing is texting or scrolling online), obstruct the mirror, disrupt someone's set, groan or scream loudly, drop weights (including heavy deadlifts or rack pulls), offer unsolicited advice, train bare-footed, stare at people, leave stuff lying around, start stripping weights off a machine unless you are sure the person before you has finished using it.

Home gyms

These days there is an increasing number of people who prefer to train from home, including some heavy hitting powerlifters. Home gyms have numerous benefits over commercial gyms. Your home gym is never closed, doesn't operate shorter opening hours at the weekend or on bank holidays, will never be too busy for you to get on the kit you need to use and will never be inaccessible due to inclement weather. You can train whilst also cooking a roast dinner or having to stay at home with poorly children. You can choose what music is played, all day, every day!

When the public gyms were closed during the COVID lockdowns, online sales of gym equipment went through the roof with many retailers selling out of most items within a matter of days. People adapted wherever possible in order to continue with their passion for lifting. Some built gyms inside their house, garage or shed or just outdoors in their garden. Some, like myself, started outdoors and subsequently moved indoors to avoid the dark, wet and cold British winter. The online community of home gym users grew exponentially in no time at all, with people all too happy to show off their home gym ideas and DIY hacks for variations of otherwise very expensive kit. Now that gyms have reopened many people have put their home gym kit up for sale and there are often good bargains still to be had. I still maintain my home gym and use it when life gets in the way of getting to my regular training facility (which is at least once per week).

You don't actually need that much equipment to get started and even with a very limited amount of space you can create a better powerlifting training set-up than is available at the majority of gyms. All you really need is a decent power rack (or half rack if space is limited), a solid FID (flat, incline, decline) bench, a standard barbell (specialist bars can be added later), somewhere to deadlift (preferably use a platform designed for this purpose and make sure the flooring is appropriate to support this activity), a decent range of (preferably) competition spec plates, and associated kit such as resistance bands, chains, kettlebells, dumbbell(s)/handles, etc. A full power rack is preferred from a safety perspective because you will most likely be training alone and they are more versatile and easy to customize with accessory items, so you will be able to do considerably more in a limited space. Depending on how much space you have you can include other bits of kit as you wish.

Some tips:
- Look for a rack with plate storage pegs.
- Do not go for the cheapest option because you get what you pay for.
- Make sure you check the maximum loading for bars and racks.
- Make sure the rack is tall enough for you to set up for squats. In some half racks the highest j-cup setting can be a little too low for taller lifters.
- Buy the best (power) bar you can afford. It should weigh 20 kg, have a centre

knurling (for squat) and the shaft should be 28–29 mm thick (as per a competition spec bar).

- Avoid bumper plates. They are too thick and you can quickly run out of room to add weight to the bar as you get stronger.
- Avoid hexagonal plates at all costs – they are no good for deadlifts.
- Look for a bench with a height close to a competition spec bench. You might also want to look for a bench that has the option to add leg curl and preacher pad attachments at a later date.

Personal kit

There are certain items that will assist you with your training, though it will not be necessary to purchase all of these at the outset. Indeed, if you are heavily overweight and want to use powerlifting as a means of weight loss (see my book: *Escape the Fat Trap: its not rocket science!*) then you might want to wait until you have lost much of your excess body fat so you don't need to purchase everything all over again in a smaller size.

Of course, if you are going to compete then you will need to use approved brands and specifications, which will cost considerably more than non-approved. Your federation will have a list of approved kit online, so make sure you check it before you buy. The IPF list is updated every four years and as of 2023 they are planning to include links to photographs of each approved item. If you fail to have approved kit at a competition then you will not be able to participate.

As well as price point, other factors that need to be taken into consideration when selecting kit include the quality of product, comfort, and will it do the job you want it to? My advice would be to go for approved kit and to buy the best you can possibly afford. "Buy once, cry once," as the saying goes. I have often purchased a cheaper option only to need to buy something more expensive subsequently, which could have been avoided if I'd bought the best to begin with. It is worth looking for second hand kit on sites such as ebay, Facebook Marketplace, Vinted, etc. as it pops up very frequently and is often as good as new for half the price!

Footwear

Your feet are all important because they form the sole interface between your body plus its heavy load and the floor, so having appropriate footwear for your training is extremely important. Your footwear needs to provide stability while also facilitating the efficiency of your various lifts. Hence, you may find yourself using different footwear for the different lifts. Regardless of the lift your feet must form a stable base in contact with the floor. It is best to visualize each foot as a tripod (the base of the little toe, the base of big toe, and the heel) and to focus on displacing the pressure evenly across these three places when setting up to lift. Once you have achieved your stable base you need to maintain it throughout the lift because any instability will likely lead to some degree of poor positioning at some point in the movement. At no point during the lift should your foot move, i.e. the foot should not rotate about the heel, the heel should not come off the ground, the toes or sides should not rock off the ground.

With the above in mind, we can now consider different types of footwear. Most training shoes have a distinctly raised heel and internal cushioning. Raised heels can be useful for those with limited ankle mobility, but they also have the potential to offset your balance as a result of tilting you forwards slightly (especially when coming out of the hole during the squat) and obviously the higher the sole at the rear then the greater this effect. If you choose a shoe with a heel, then the heel must not exceed 5 cm in height.

Any degree of internal cushioning will form an unstable base when you set up for a lift. The last thing you want is to be bouncing around on raised and cushioned soles whilst trying to remain stable with a heavy weight on your back. Another disadvantage of a high sole is that you will need to pull the barbell up further during the deadlift. It is worth checking the width of the sole before you make a decision. Some shoes have relatively narrow soles, no different to standard training shoes, whereas others have soles that extend outwards slightly at the heel and around the midfoot. I have tried both and the latter create a much more stable interface with the floor.

Shoes do not need to be of an approved brand for competition, so there are plenty of options and there are online reviews comparing those available to help you choose. Hiking shoes/boots are not allowed. Deadlift slippers can be worn for deadlifts, though some of the more flimsy ones are not recommended if lifting sumo style. For bench press the main concern is having a decent grip on the sole so that your feet do not slip when engaging leg drive. A specialist lifting shoe with a wide toe-box was recently released in limited numbers by Squat University and this has had some excellent feedback.

Powerlifting belt

The main purpose of wearing a belt is not to support your lower back as most people assume. Rather, it functions to provide an unyielding surface against which you can brace your abdominal muscles in order to generate core stability and rigidity. Hence, powerlifting belts require a broad surface area all the way around (not just at the back as seen in traditional weightlifting belts) and function better if worn higher up around the abdomen, where you can generate a greater intra-abdominal force with which to press against it.

How often you wear your belt is very much down to personal preference, but a common rule of thumb is to use it only when the weights you are lifting are equal to or greater than 90% of the maximum lift you can do for one repetition (your 1RM, or one-rep-max), because it is important to develop 'unassisted' core body strength and stability. That said, you will come across some people shifting extremely heavy weights who prefer not to use a belt at all and you will see others using one for much lighter weights than 90% of their 1RM. Some people will use a belt whilst bench pressing (remember it is a full-body lift!) whereas others will not. As you will have started to gather by now, it is usually the case that there is no one-size-fits-all rule, so just do what feels right for you. You will no doubt meet people who will tell you that you should not wear a belt at all because it stops you building up your core strength – ignore them! Bracing into a belt correctly requires some practice, so make sure you do some research on this (there are plenty of useful articles online) and seek advice from other heavy lifters that you see using a belt.

There are several types of fastening mechanisms, from the traditional one or two-prong and hole design, to Velcro fasteners (not allowed at competition), quick release buckle mechanism and steel lever buckle mechanisms. The lever buckles permit super quick opening and closing, which is great for competitions because the last thing you want to be doing is wasting time and effort struggling to fasten your belt tight enough when you should be focusing on your imminent lift. The same is true of regular training, so my advice would be to opt for this type of belt.

With most lever belts you need to unscrew (reposition and then screw back in again) part of the fitting in order to adjust the tightness of the belt. Consequently, this type of buckle is not particularly useful if you are likely to want to adjust between medium-tight (e.g. for warm-ups) and very tight fittings (for new PBs) during a competition. There are other lever belts that can be adjusted very quickly without having to unscrew anything (e.g. SBD). These are expensive, but are worth the cost. The IPF belt specifications are 10 cm wide (maximum) and up to 13 mm thick.

Wrist wraps

Wrist wraps serve to provide wrist joint stability, but when wrapped over the back of the hand, they also maintain a straight forearm–hand alignment by preventing the hand from bending backwards at the wrist. This is important when setting up for both the squat and the bench press (and also overhead press). When applying the wraps the aim is to immobilize your wrist such that your hand cannot move forwards, backwards or sideways.

In the squat, a straight forearm–hand alignment reduces strain on the elbow and in the bench press the straight alignment means the weight of the bar will be stacked directly above the long bones of your forearm. This position provides the greatest possible support, rather than having the weight bend your wrists backwards and downwards, which can put excessive strain on the relatively weak wrist joint.

There is also a benefit to applying wrist wraps tightly around the wrist for deadlifts because they cause your fingers to squeeze the bar more tightly, improving your grip strength slightly. In this case, do not wrap around the back of the hand. Start at the base of the hand and wrap snugly around the wrist whilst tightly clenching your fist. You will need to release the wraps between lifts in order to restore blood flow.

The IPF technical rules state that wraps must not exceed 1 m in length or 8 cm in width. Most wraps have a thumb-loop which can be used as an aid when securing them, but this loop is not allowed to be over the thumb or fingers during an actual competition lift. The affixed wrap must not extend beyond 10 cm above and 2 cm below the centre of the wrist joint and must not exceed a covering width of 12 cm.

Neoprene knee and elbow sleeves

The purpose of knee sleeves is to stabilize the knee joint and to provide light compression and warmth to promote blood flow and reduce the risk of inflammatory conditions such as tendonitis. Over the longer term, they can also slow the onset of more serious and chronic knee ailments. They feel good during heavy squats and their elasticity gives the feeling of helping you 'out of the hole', but to what extent they really do this is difficult to quantify. I also wear them when doing deadlifts, again for the support they provide, but they also have the added bonus of protecting the top of the knee from being accidentally bashed when lowering the bar with a heavy load on it, as can happen on occasion.

You may see two different size guides when ordering them: 1. regular/comfortable fit, 2. tight/competition fit, based on the measurement around the centre of the knee. I would suggest opting for the second option, but getting them on can be tricky and there is a special technique to doing this. Identify the correct (left vs right) sleeve from the label inside. Roll down the top of the sleeve and roll up the bottom of the sleeve then slip it over the foot. Straighten your leg and using two hands pull the sleeve upwards. This needs to be done rather firmly. If you stop midway then it is a bit awkward (but not impossible) to get it moving again. Once in place, roll back the top and roll down the bottom. They feel very strange at first, especially when you try to walk in them but you soon get used to it. Make sure you turn them inside out and air (or preferably wash) them after use because they do get hot and sweaty!

During competition the sleeves must be centred over the knee and the bottom of the sleeves must not be in contact with the top of the socks. The Technical Controller will reject any knee sleeves that have been put on the lifter with the assistance of any other person or method, e.g. by using plastic slidings, lubricants, etc.

Elbow sleeves may also be a useful option for the same reasons as knee sleeves. I have certainly found them beneficial in the treatment and avoidance of elbow tendonitis. However, elbow sleeves are not allowed in competition so make sure you train without them in your run up to the meet so that you can judge your opening lifts accordingly.

Other attire: Singlet, t-shirt, socks, underwear

You can pretty much wear whatever you like for training and you will no doubt see a considerable range of fashions being paraded at any gym you walk into. There are just a few provisos. First, your clothing should allow you to conduct your lifts without any hindrance in terms of restricting your movement. Second, it is advisable not to have a bare upper back and shoulders when training the squat, in order to protect your skin from the knurling on the bar. Long-sleeved compression tops (and leggings if you like) are beneficial in that they keep your joints and muscles warm throughout your training. If you wear a hooded top, make sure you wear the hood up when doing the squat, otherwise it will create an unstable surface for the bar to rest on.

For a formal powerlifting competition a one-piece singlet over a plain t-shirt and knee-length socks are required. The tight attire allows the judges to easily see if you have made a legal lift (if you are wearing baggy shorts or tracksuits then it can be very difficult to determine if a squat has gone deep enough to count or whether you have raised your bum off the bench whilst pressing). To this end, it has been suggested by some that an all-black singlet can produce little in the way of shadow/contrast at the hip crease during the squat and so a lighter colour or a singlet with a stripe or straight line demarcation between colours may be advantageous for those who aim to squat only as deep as they need to.

For competition, the t-shirt must not consist of any rubberized or similar stretch material, nor have any reinforced seams or pockets, buttons, zippers other than around the neck collar. The sleeves must terminate between the lifter's deltoid muscle and the lifter's elbow. It should be plain with no logos or emblems, apart from (if desired) that of the lifter's nation, the lifter's name, the lifter's IPF region, or the event in which the lifter is competing, as per the "Sponsor's Logos" in the IPF rule book. At national and lower level contests only, the shirt may include the lifter's club or individual sponsor. Any such emblems or logos must be printed or embroidered and be no larger than 5 cm x 2 cm.

The purpose of the long (knee-length) socks is to protect your shins from being scraped by the bar during deadlifts. The rough surface (knurling) of the bar can lead to nasty scratching and bleeding of the shins. The last thing you want to do is pick up a bar covered in somebody else's blood, so it is not just about your own protection, it is also for the consideration of others who will be using the bar after you have finished. Socks may be of any colour or brand and may bear manufacturer's logos.

In terms of underwear, a standard commercial "athletic supporter" or standard commercial briefs (but not boxer shorts) of any mixture of cotton, nylon or polyester can be worn. Women may also wear a commercial or sports bra. Swimming trunks or any item consisting of rubberized or similar stretch material except in the waistband, are not permitted (the IPF rule book includes images for reference – as a good rule of thumb, avoid underwear deemed to have 'legs'). No supportive undergarments are allowed at IPF competitions.

In addition to the kit discussed above, female Muslim lifters may wear a Hijab (head scarf) while lifting at competition. However, the Jury or Referees may ask the lifter to fix her hair accordingly in order to perform the bench press to competition standard. It is also permitted to wear a non-supportive full-body suit or combination of leggings and/or long-sleeved top, along with the IPF required apparel by those who wish to dress more modestly, whether that be for religious or personal reasons. Although the rule book (as of March 2023) has not been updated to include this information, the minutes of the 2020 British Powerlifting AGM (Section 12.12) show the motion presenting this proposal was passed. This was reaffirmed at the BP AGM 2023 and the IPF confirmed this in a statement, noting that there was no need to give advance warning or notice to competition organizers or referees.

Resistance bands

Thick rubber resistance bands are commonplace in gyms these days, though not all gyms supply them and you may need to purchase your own should you decide to use them. They range in thickness and strength and are often colour coded accordingly. You may see people using them attached to bars when doing any of the lifts prescribed in this book. In this case, the resistance bands alter the amount of weight that you are supporting yourself as the bar moves through the range of the lift. For example, if used during a squat with the bands supporting the bar from above, when you unrack the bar and step back to the start position you are taking the full weight of the bar, but as you descend, an increasing amount of the weight is taken up by the resistance bands as they stretch. Similarly, if they are used during a deadlift and are attached to the bar from the bottom, then as you pull the bar upwards the stretching of the bands actually increases the weight that you are pulling.

If you intend to use bands in this way (and you should once you pass beyond the novice and early intermediate stages) then you will need two of each colour, one for each side of the barbell. Make sure the bands are evenly spaced on the bar and that any racks or other equipment you attach the bands to are firmly attached to the wall, floor etc. as a heavily laden barbell can cause even a heavy rack to topple over, which is never a good idea if you are beneath the bar. I also find it useful to have a thin resistance band (usually red in colour), which can be used to assist with shoulder mobility exercises and general warming up at the start of training sessions or at competition.

Chalk

The chalk is applied to the hands for the purpose of soaking up moisture from sweat and to enhance grip strength through increased friction resulting in heavier PBs. It certainly makes the connection between the skin and bar feel much more secure when moving heavy loads. Some lifters also have chalk applied to their upper back region in order to increase friction and help stop the bar from slipping during squats and also to prevent slipping on the bench during the bench press. Do not apply chalk to your legs for deadlifts! The white powder you will see some people covered in for deadlifts at competition is talc, which has the opposite effect of chalk. Weightlifter's (or gymnast's) chalk can be purchased in powder, block or even liquid form. However, many gyms do not allow the use of liquid chalk because it can be very hard to clean off the bars and this is fair enough. If you use regular chalk take care not to make a large mess all over the gym that somebody else will be expected to clear up! Regular chalk is usually provided at competitions (though rarely in the warm-up room!), liquid chalk is not permitted.

Hair

At competition it is important that your hairstyle does not obscure the back of your head when lying down on the bench and the Jury or referees may ask you to fix your hair accordingly. For those with long pony tails take care when squatting. I have seen several examples of people failing a squat attempt and as they try to dump the bar off their back it somehow manages to trap the hair yanking the lifter down backwards at the same time. This must be a very unpleasant experience.

A note on lifting gloves

Gloves do very little other than prevent calluses forming and certainly do not do anything to increase your grip strength. They are not permitted at competition and if you do decide to wear them during training expect people to talk about you behind your back!

Programming for Beginners

The basic principle

Whenever your body is exposed to a form of physical **stress** it responds to it. This response consists of two elements: **recovery** and **adaptation**. The greater the stress, the longer your body takes to recover and adapt. Repeating the cycle of stress-recovery-adaptation is how you get stronger, but few people appreciate or understand this very simple principle. They assume that working out in the gym has a direct and immediate effect on strength and muscle size, but this is not the case. Consequently, they tend to neglect their rest and recovery and by doing so will lose much of the benefit of having trained in the first place. Your workout provides the stress, but the adaptation occurs during the recovery period (especially while you are asleep), which is why **the amount of rest you get is extremely important**. The speed and degree of recovery will also be assisted by consuming plenty of protein (in an overall calorie surplus) and lots of water.

There is a second very important element which is that the stress applied (i.e. the weights lifted) needs to be increased each time you train in order to drive further adaptation (=strength). This principle is known as **progressive overload**. If you do not constantly increase the stress then the body will stop adapting and no additional progress will be made. You will see many people in the gym who shift the same weights for the same number of reps and the same number of sets week after week and month after month. They are exercising rather than training and will not make any significant progress by doing this.

The further you progress in strength training, the greater the stress you will be exerting on your body each time you train. As you progress from the novice stage, through the intermediate and advanced stages your recovery time will need to be increased in order to allow the required adaptation to take place. As has been noted repeatedly up until this point, everybody is different so you will need to use the following as a guide in order to determine what works best for you. Certainly, you should be able to progress through the novice stage as directed without any problems and you will be surprised at how quickly you make great progress. However, when it comes to the intermediate stage the situation becomes more complicated because there are different variables that you will be able to manipulate in order to drive progress, such as rep and set numbers, speed of reps, pause between reps, rest between sets and rest between training sessions. So long as your manipulation of the variables constantly increases the overall stress imposed, then this will serve to drive your strength gains.

Finally, you need to be **consistent** with your training. If you do not turn up to train then you will not get stronger, it is as simple as that. Your training slots need to be non-negotiable – training needs to be more a part of who you are, rather than just something that you do. Make it intrinsic to the success of your day. I set my alarm for 4:45 am every day (but am often awake by 4:30 am) in order to get to the gym by 5:45 am. If I train while my wife and three kids are still asleep there is no chance of them interrupting my focus or curtailing my plans. It does not matter so much that my cats wake up at the same time as me because they are (marginally) less demanding than my wife and kids.

Acclimatization stage

Before getting started with the formal lifting program you will need to spend as long as is required in order to make sure you are able to conduct each lift through the full range of motion as defined by competition standards, whilst using the most efficient and effective technique as defined by your own personal biomechanics (anthropometry). If you initially lack the mobility to achieve an appropriate range of motion for a particular lift, e.g. not hitting depth in the squat, or unable to set up the deadlift, then start with accessory exercises to address the particular problem. In the scenarios above you could employ box squats for the squat depth limitation and block or rack pulls to gradually work closer to the correct deadlift set up.

Moreover, you need to ingrain these motor patterns such that all subsequent reps can be performed to the same standard. There is no point increasing weight on the bar until this has been achieved, so the focus here needs to be on technique rather than load. Once you are confident in doing this you can proceed to the novice or linear progression stage.

When done correctly, lifting should not hurt! However, you may experience pain despite using the correct technique and you will often hear people in the gym complaining that their shoulder hurts when they bench, their back hurts when they deadlift or they feel pain in their hips when they squat. This may manifest itself at the beginning of your training or may appear further down the line as a result of form creep (see page 56) or poor technique on assistance exercises leading to impingement of one form or another. This is a painful condition caused by rubbing or pressure on a tendon, nerve, etc., by adjacent structures and is an issue that should be dealt with sooner rather than later. Some simple physical preparation mobility drills prior to training the lift will usually be sufficient to resolve the problem.

Linear progression (novice) stage

When you first start training you will be performing each lift for three sets of five repetitions (reps), with a pause between sets, so this equals 15 reps in total for each lift. You will not be strong enough to stress your body too much and recovery and adaptation will take place very quickly (within a day or two). This means you will be able to easily train each lift twice per week, with a few days rest in between, whilst also increasing the stress (in this case the amount of weight moved) each time. This needs to be done gradually, so you are stressing your body just a little bit more each time. In most gyms the lightest free weight is a 1.25 kg disc, so adding one of these to each side of the bar will represent an increase of 2.5 kg each time and adding this amount is fine for bench press (and overhead press, added in here as an additional compound lift for building upper body strength). You should be able to add 2.5 kg either side for your squats and deadlifts. If you try to add a lot more weight too quickly you will slow down your progress and risk injuring yourself.

A simple novice routine may look like this:

WEEK 1: MONDAY				
Exercise	Reps	Sets	Weight	Cumulative +kg
Warm-up				
Squat	5	3		
Bench press	5	3		
Deadlift	5	3		

WEEK 1: WEDNESDAY				
Exercise	Reps	Sets	Weight	Cumulative +kg
Warm-up				
Squat	5	3	+5kg	5kg
Overhead press	5	3		
Accessory 1	8	3		
Accessory 2	8	3		
Core training				

WEEK 1: FRIDAY				
Exercise	Reps	Sets	Weight	Cumulative +kg
Warm-up				
Deadlift	5	3	+5kg	5kg
Bench press	5	3	+2.5kg	2.5kg
Accessory 1	8	3		
Accessory 2	8	3		
Core training				

WEEK 2: MONDAY				
Exercise	Reps	Sets	Weight	Cumulative +kg
Warm-up				
Squat	5	3	+5kg	10kg
Bench press	5	3	+2.5kg	5kg
Deadlift	5	3	+5kg	10kg

WEEK 2: WEDNESDAY				
Exercise	Reps	Sets	Weight	Cumulative +kg
Warm-up				
Squat	5	3	+5kg	10kg
Overhead press	5	3	+2.5kg	2.5kg
Accessory 1	8	3		
Accessory 2	8	3		
Core training				

WEEK 2: FRIDAY				
Exercise	Reps	Sets	Weight	Cumulative +kg
Warm-up				
Deadlift	5	3	+5kg	15kg
Bench press	5	3	+2.5kg	7.5kg
Accessory 1	8	3		
Accessory 2	8	3		
Core training				

WEEK 3: MONDAY				
Exercise	Reps	Sets	Weight	Cumulative +kg
Warm-up				
Squat	5	3	+5kg	15kg
Bench press	5	3	+2.5kg	10kg
Deadlift	5	3	+5kg	20kg

WEEK 3: WEDNESDAY				
Exercise	Reps	Sets	Weight	Cumulative +kg
Warm-up				
Squat	5	3	+5kg	20kg
Overhead press	5	3	+2.5kg	5kg
Accessory 1	8	3		
Accessory 2	8	3		
Core training				

Using this approach will lead to steady progress in the amount of weight you can move for each lift. Indeed, if you were to plot your progress over time on a graph the increase in weight lifted would follow a straight line, with a slight slope in an upward direction, which is why this is known as the **linear progression** stage. This is exactly what you are seeking to achieve. Obviously, this linear progression cannot continue indefinitely and the period for which it is realistically possible varies from person to person. You may be able to manage it for three to six months or you may be able to keep going for longer. Ultimately, the longer you can keep the novice, linear progression stage running the better!

However, there will come a time when you start missing reps in the second and/or third sets and this might be a sign that you are coming towards the end of your novice phase. You will now be very close to the margins of your physical abilities and you will need to work much harder to keep the linear progression running for a little while longer. Really push yourself here … focus everything you have on completing each set, develop a healthy aggression towards the bar and show it who is the boss! Really fire yourself up before you get under it. Increasing your rest periods between sets will help for a while. Eventually though the bar will get the better of you and your progress will stop if you do not do something different to continue driving it along. This is called hitting a plateau – your upward sloping trend line will start to level off. This happens to everybody and so long as you are aware of its inevitability and are prepared for it, then it will not be a problem because all it signifies is that you are about to enter the next training phase.

If you feel yourself getting very tired it may simply be a case that you are not getting enough calories inside you to drive the amount of work you are asking your body to do, or it may be the result of accumulated fatigue (both muscular and CNS), which will set in over time. In the latter case it is worth adding in a **deload week** to help you recover from the fatigue whilst keeping your body going through the motions of doing the lifts. Simply reduce the weights on all lifts down to around 80% and complete all your weekly sets as normal, but at the reduced weight. Then start off again where you left off the week before. Some people will suggest that you should deload every four to six weeks. Others suggest doing it as and when you feel it is necessary. It comes down to personal preference. If you really do not feel the need to deload then there is not much likely to be gained by doing it. You will soon get the hang of interpreting your bodily needs correctly, in terms of whether you just need a few more calories (and do not be afraid to add these at this time!) or whether you should incorporate a deload week.

Keep things as simple as possible during the novice stage and do not venture to the intermediate stage until you have absolutely exhausted the linear phase increases! Remember, the ultimate aim of the novice lifter is to train with the least amount of complexity for the biggest return on time and effort for the longest possible period of time.

The intermediate stage

In terms of traditional training programming classification this stage follows the novice stage and precedes the advanced stage, which in turn is followed by the elite stage. Most trainees will never reach the advanced stage because they continue to progress as an intermediate for such a long time. Moreover, if you attempt to employ advanced training techniques too early on in your lifting career, you will most likely experience suboptimal gains, burnout and injury.

Given the purpose of the current book, advanced and elite training theory will not be discussed in depth here, and there are plenty of other resources available for those who would like to delve into this later. Again, you will be repeating the cycle of stress-recovery-adaptation using the principle of progressive overload in order to develop strength, followed by a peaking phase leading up to competition or when attempting new PBs. However, there are many more variables that can be manipulated, rather than just the weight on the bar (as in the novice stage).

During this phase training can be considered as a perpetual experiment in self-improvement as you try and work out how much to lift and how often to lift in order to maximize new strength gains and push through plateaus. For example, taking both extremes of your strength range you could squat 20% of your 1RM every day or even squat your 1RM every day, but neither approach would result in any gains. As a rule, intensity (weight lifted) is more important than frequency, so the question then becomes, how often can I lift heavy and still recover enough to develop more strength? Continuing with squats as an example, a novice can easily lift three times per week as they practice and perfect their technique. Once proficient and they start to lift heavier and more taxing weights, the frequency will need to decrease to two times per week (usually between three and six months) and as future progress is made frequency may need to drop to once per week. Even lifting just once per week, this process cannot continue indefinitely, so you will need to start periodizing your training into different 'blocks' through manipulation of the various different training variables available to you.

Training variables

Volume and intensity are the two main components of your strength training program, which can be manipulated to drive strength gains. Volume relates to numbers of reps and sets, whereas intensity concerns the amount of weight lifted per rep. Clearly, if you can do a set of five reps at 100 kg, you should be able to accomplish just a single rep (**intensity**) at a weight greater than this. Conversely, if you wanted to knock out a set of eight reps (**volume**) then you would need to lower the weight in order to accomplish it. There are plenty of apps available to give you an idea of how much weight it should be possible to move at different rep ranges based on your current abilities. In the above scenario you could be expected to lift a single rep (intensity) of around 113 kg, but for a set of eight reps (volume) you would need to reduce the weight to around 91 kg.

In the novice stage it was recommended to lift three sets of five reps for the top working set in each training session. Whilst this approach is fine for the novice stage, for building muscle (hypertrophy work) training multiple top sets of the same weight does not necessarily work so well for intermediate strength programming. This is because it will be easier to generate greater focus and effort into just a single top working set and thus allow for a slightly greater intensity when compared with multiple top sets. Nonetheless, it is worth noting that five is a rather magical number when it comes to number of reps and strength development. Hence, it is always good to aim for a top set of five reps and when the weights get too heavy for this you can incorporate **cluster sets** with minimal rest between rep clusters, e.g. 4+1 reps, 3+2 reps, 3+1+1 reps, etc. You can keep driving this until you are able to hit five reps without a rest and then increase the weights and start again.

Additional training variables that can be manipulated include: the length of your training cycle, weight increments, number of work sets, number of reps per set, speed of reps, rest period between sets, the type of program/cycle (see below), frequency of training, lift set up (e.g. sumo vs conventional for deadlift; high-bar vs low-bar vs safety-bar for squats, grip width or touch-and-go vs paused reps for bench, as just a few examples). Indeed, just to give an example of how much variation is actually available to you, consider the bench press. It can be performed as regular, declined or inclined (3 variations). Each of these variations can be performed using a wide, standard or narrow grip (3x3 = 9 variations). Each of these 9 variations can be performed with or without bands or chains (9x3 = 27 variations). These can be performed for strength (high intensity) or hypertrophy (high volume) (= 54 variations), with a regular bar, a duffalo bar or a football bar (54x3 = 162 variations) ... and so on. I expect you have got the idea by now.

Given all these different variables and potential combinations, the intermediate phase of training can be a great place to experiment with different training protocols. However, the flip side of this is that it becomes easy to get lost in the freedom of possibilities and fall victim to the trap of program hopping. Too often people will be impatient and switch from one program to another without allowing sufficient time for any of them to pay dividends and then wonder why they are not making any progress. Once you have decided on a particular program it is important that you stick with it for at least 12 weeks before giving up on it.

If using percentage-based (of your 1RM) training programs, you may need to use combinations of fractional or micro-plates (small weight plates ranging from 0.25 to 0.5 kg) in order to get the correct weight on the bar. These may not be available in your gym, but you can purchase them quite cheaply (or expensively) online.

Some examples of intermediate routines

The following table shows examples of different cycles that can be used to help stop your strength gains from stalling. The values are based on a hypothetical lifter with a squat (or deadlift) 5RM of 100kg (if it were a bench press example the weight increments would be 2.5kg rather than 5kg) and the shaded cells represent new 5RM PBs.

Week	4-Week Power	12-Week Wave	2-Step	4-Week V-L-H
1	90kg × 5	85kg × 5	87.5kg × 5	Wk1-Mon: Volume
2	95kg × 5	90kg × 5	87.5kg × 5	Wk1-Wed: Light
3	100kg × 5	95kg × 5	92.5kg × 5	Wk1-Fri: Heavy
4	105kg × 5 PB	90kg × 5	92.5kg × 5	Wk2-Mon: Volume
5	92.5kg × 5	95kg × 5	97.5kg × 5	Wk2-Wed: Light
6	97.5kg × 5	100kg × 5	97.5kg × 5	Wk2-Fri: Heavy
7	102.5kg × 5	95kg × 5	102.5kg × 5 PB	Wk3-Mon: Volume
8	107.5kg × 5 PB	100kg × 5	102.5kg × 5	Wk3-Wed: Light
9	95kg × 5	105kg × 5 PB	107.5kg × 5 PB	Wk3-Fri: Heavy
10	100kg × 5	100kg × 5	107.5kg × 5	Wk4-Mon: Volume
11	105kg × 5	105kg × 5	112.5kg × 5 PB	Wk4-Wed: Light
12	110kg × 5 PB	110kg × 5 PB	112.5kg × 5	Wk4-Fri: Heavy

The four-week power program results in a PB every fourth week, after which the weight drops back to slightly heavier than the original starting weight and the four-week cycle is repeated, with slightly heavier weights each time. This program can be drawn out to 6, 8, 10 or even12 weeks.

The wave program consists of two increment weeks followed by a fall-back week, then two increment weeks followed by a fall-back week and so it continues.

The step cycle program involves repeating the same weight for two consecutive training sessions before increasing the load. The idea is that the second time you lift the same weight it should feel easier and you can apply the principle of progressive overload by increasing the speed of the reps if possible.

The four-week **V**olume-**L**ight-**H**eavy cycle essentially uses a volume session at the beginning of the week to drive a new intensity PB at the end of the week, with a light session in between.

The key to all of the above is to select an appropriate starting weight. It must not be too light that it does not impose a sufficient stress to drive adaptation and it must not be too heavy, such that you stall before reaching a new PB. Starting at around 80–85% of your RM is a good place to start.

5-3-1

This is a simple but effective program suitable for most intermediate lifters, which results in strength gains and minimizes plateaus. It runs in cycles of four weeks, with the fourth week being a deload week. Because it starts light and progresses relatively slowly the deload weeks are optional for the first and second cycles. This program trains the three competition lifts (squat, bench press and deadlift) and the overhead press, once per week and working off percentages of your 1RM (which can be calculated from submaximal weights using an online 1RM calculator). If you do not have an app handy you can use the Epley 1RM formula, which estimates your maximum single lift intensity (1RM) based on the number of reps (r) lifted of a lesser weight (w). The formula is: $1RM = w(1 + r/30)$. When using a RM calculator anything from 10RM and lower is fairly accurate at predicting a 1RM – obviously, the lower the RM input, the more accurate the 1RM output will be.

The sets, reps and percentage values are shown in the table below. The third and final working set for each session (except the download week) consists of as many reps as possible (AMRAP) above the minimum target value stated.

Week	Warm-up %1RM	Reps per set	Weights %1RM
1	36/45/54 for 5/5/3 reps	5/5/AMRAP>5	59/68/77
2		3/3/AMRAP>3	63/72/81
3		5/3/AMRAP>1	68/77/86
4 (deload)	N/A	5/5/5	36/45/54

You will train four times each week as follows: Monday (squats), Tuesday (bench press), Wednesday (rest day), Thursday (deadlift), Friday (overhead press), Saturday and Sunday (rest days). Once you have run the full cycle of three weeks (or four weeks if you include the deload) add 2.5 kg to your now theoretical 1RM value for bench press and overhead press and recalculate the weights to be lifted, again using the percentage values in the table above. Do the same for squats and deadlifts, but use a 5 kg increment. Keep these cycles running for as long as possible.

In this program you also train two accessory lifts per session, alternating between light and heavy weeks. Feel free to mix up your accessories in order to add variation to your training or, when necessary, focus your accessories towards specific weak points of your lifts.

Volume–Strength–Power–Peak cycles

A common approach for an initial intermediate routine is to break your training down into Volume–Strength–Power–Peak blocks, which can be implemented in a variety of ways.

The volume can be used as a driver for intensity over both the short term and the long term. In the first example, volume (e.g. five sets of 10 reps at 70% of the weight where you finished at the end of the linear increment stage) can be used early in the week to drive one set of five reps of intensity later in the week. You will still add 1.25 kg to each side of the bar every time you manage 5 sets of 10 for the volume and 1 set of 5 for the intensity. By doing this it should be possible to keep the intensity increasing (whilst still maintaining 5 reps) week after week, which is the ultimate aim. However, the volume may start to slow down and as you increase the weights, you might start hitting sets of 9, 8, 7 or 6 reps. Don't worry about this. Keep the weight the same the following week and just make sure you improve on the number of reps in at least one (but preferably all) sets (using cluster sets if need be). So long as the intensity is still increasing, the volume is doing its job. Eventually you will hit all volume sets for 10 uninterrupted reps and then you can increase the weight again. If the fatigue becomes too much you can extend your cycle over more than a week and include a light session between the volume and the intensity sets (e.g. Day 1: volume, Day 4: light sets, Day 8: intensity, Day 12: start again).

You might be surprised at how different the volume training is. It is a bit like doing weighted cardio, in that it really gets your heart beating and leaves you short of breath. Be certain to allow yourself sufficient rest periods between sets in order to allow your basal breathing and heart rates to return close to normal. Overall, this can be a very taxing part of the training cycle because you are really pushing both your volume and your intensity.

A longer-term approach using the same philosophy is to use a periodization cycle of four phases, which shifts gradually over several months from high volume at low intensity to low volume at high intensity in order to achieve new peak levels of strength. If each stage is run for three weeks followed by a two-week peak and deload at the end this periodization routine can be run three times over one year. Aim to start this program 14 weeks before competition day so that the you aim to finish your peak on competition day itself.

Volume driving strength potential – hypertrophy

Having larger muscles does not necessarily mean that you have greater strength. You will see plenty of non-bulky people shifting very heavy weights, which some more muscular people would be unable to move. Nonetheless, having larger muscles does increase your potential for developing additional strength and that is the principle behind this phase of the program.

In this phase you will be doing two days of volume training per lift (just one day for the deadlift as this takes longer to recover from) and no intensity training. Start with the weight at 65% of your 1 rep max for five sets of 10 reps and gradually increase the weight throughout this training period so you finish close to 75% of your 1RM for five sets of 10 reps. Try to keep the rest period between sets at no more than two minutes.

Realizing the strength potential

This is the so-called strength block. In the previous phase the aim was to increase muscle size, whereas here the aim here is to develop increased muscle strength. Start at 75% of your 1RM and increase gradually until you reach 85% of your 1RM. Aim for six reps per set for three sets. Take up to five minutes rest between sets in order to give your muscles sufficient time to recover. Again, try and train each lift (apart from the deadlift) twice per week, but if becomes too much reduce training to once per week for all lifts.

Generating more power

The power phase consists of five sets of low repetitions (three) and with intensity (weight) levels gradually increasing from 86% to 93% of your 1RM, training each lift just once per week for four weeks. The rest period between sets during this phase may need to be extended because heavy power reps can be very taxing.

Peak phase (applies to all programs)

This is the stage where all the foregoing comes together and you should be seeking to hit new PBs on all your lifts. The goal is to adjust your training program such that you reduce the muscular and CNS fatigue accrued from training while maintaining the strength adaptations. The most effective way to do this is to keep the intensity high and the volume low. This phase will last for two to three weeks (though more advanced lifters may peak for longer) and will ideally be planned so that the final peak falls on competition day, following which you will take a week or two as a deload break in order to recover.

There are numerous different strategies that can be employed here ranging from an immediate drop down to 30% of your total volume for all lifts, or the reduction process can be transitioned gradually in a linear fashion. For example, you could drop your volume by 20% weekly over three weeks for a total decrease of 60%, or do a slower taper by decreasing volume 10% over four to six weeks for the same total decrease of volume. Another option is to drop volume in a non-linear fashion, such that you form a curve, which can be achieved by, for example, dropping 20% on the first week, followed by 15% of the previous week on the second week, followed by 10% of the previous week on the third week, followed by 5% of the previous week on the fourth week. Whichever option you choose, much of this volume reduction can come by cutting out your accessory lifts so that you can maintain your focus on your competition lifts. Again, as is repeated often, everybody is unique and responds differently, so you may have to try a few different routines before you find out what works best for you. Some people do not bother to peak at all and go straight to comp from their current training block.

Remember, you still need to maintain high intensity during this stage despite dropping off the volume. The focus will be heavy triples and heavy doubles leading on to heavy singles. You also need to increase your lift specificity during this stage to focus solely on competition standard lifts, so cut out speciality bars, chains, bands, boards, etc. Make sure you train the competition commands, whether it be with a training partner/coach (preferred) or in your head. If you train wearing elbow sleeves (or other equipment) not allowed in competition then ditch these as well. In the final week of your peak, the last few training sessions should focus only on your squat and bench press competition standard lifts and nothing else and the intensity should be reduced to around 50% of your expected competition new PB. Three sets of three reps are sufficient to keep the movement patterns operating. Do not train your deadlift in the final week.

Use this time to get comfortable with your competition openers and maybe even your second attempts, but do not go beyond this. You need to save yourself for competition day. Remember, this stage is about recovering from fatigue whilst retaining your strength gains. There is not much you can do to get significantly stronger during your taper phase, but there is plenty you can do to get weaker. No amount of training at this stage will add any extra kgs to your total, but if you fail to properly program and regulate your peaking phase you will most likely wreck your competition performance potential. Essentially, any heavy training during this period will disrupt your recovery process and likely ruin your chances of having a successful meet. Common mistakes which can result in this include: trying to hit new 1RMs, reducing intensity as well as volume, making your taper too long or too short, trying to drop significant body weight at the same time, thinking too critically about your lifting technique which may lead you to want to try and tweak it … this is not the time to try new things.

Getting the competition peaking phase right is somewhat of an art-form and the more you do it the better you will become at it. If you are not competing then you will need to finish your peak by maxing out beyond your current 1RM. In this case, a potential peaking routine might look something like this:
Week 1 – 94% x 2 sets of 3 reps
Week 2 – 97% x 2 sets of 2 reps
Week 3 – 100% x 2 set of 2 reps
Week 4 – 104% x 1 set of 1 rep (new PB)
Week 5 – 108% x 1 set of 1 rep (new PB)

Intentional overreaching

The concept of intentional overreaching (also known as functional overreaching) is a powerful tool that can be used to boost strength during your peaking phase by setting in motion a process of supercompensation. In theory (not everybody agrees it works), it works by significantly increasing your current volume (double it) and intensity (increase slightly if possible) beyond what you would normally be able to sustain over one to two weeks before your peaking phase begins. By training significantly harder in this manner the supercompensation effect causes adaptations to be realized weeks after the super-heavy training sessions and hopefully coinciding with competition day. If you decide to employ this technique take extra care to focus on your form, as injuring yourself four weeks before a competition is never a good thing. You will need to increase your calories and sleep (if possible) to reap the full benefits of this approach.

Westside conjugate training

The examples so far have involved training primarily the competition lifts and manipulating other variables, such as weight, reps, sets, speed, etc. Of course this makes sense at the outset of your lifting journey because you need to perfect the lifting techniques and the best way of doing this is through repetition. It also makes sense because if you ask most people for advice on how to squat more or bench more (weight), they will tell you to squat more and bench more (volume) and this does work so long as you program it correctly.

However, the elite lifters at the infamous Westside Barbell (USA) employ a rather different technique which they named the Westside Congjugate Method, which helps them to continue progressing once they have become accommodated to high results in the classic lifts. In this system the lifters do not focus on the competition lifts, but rather variations of them (as per, but not limited to, the examples listed in the accessory lifts earlier on). The training has three main components: the dynamic method, the max effort method and the repetition method.

The focus of the dynamic method is on developing speed and explosive strength, often using bands, chains, etc. The lift is changed every three weeks, with each three week dynamic wave starting at 50% of your 1RM, increasing by 5% each week (50, 55, 60) before accounting for additional resistance supplied by the bands, chains etc. If you start too heavy you will not be able to move the bar fast enough to achieve the desired results.

The max effort session is done 72 hours after the dynamic session and the aim is to max out on that particular day with that particular lift, though it may not necessarily represent a new PB. In order to prevent training regress due to muscular and CNS breakdown the max effort lift variation trained is changed weekly.

The repetition method refers to accessory lifts used to train the core and other elements of the body such as lats, triceps, delts, back, glutes etc. for hypertrophy, which are done after the dynamic training session. These lifts are also switched around on a three-weekly basis. Switching the lifts so frequently almost completely eliminates the biological law of accommodation, which can be defined as 'a decrease in the response of an organism to a sustained stimulus' and so deload sessions are rarely required.

In order to maintain competition specific motor patterns it is a good idea to train the main lifts (squat, bench press and deadlift) once every four or five weeks on max effort day and once every third wave on dynamic effort day.

To summarize the theory, the max effort component improves absolute strength (the maximum force the athlete can produce), the dynamic component increases the speed at which that force can be generated and combining the two results in a very strong and explosive powerlifter.

For more detail on these advanced techniques see the books by Louie Simmons in the Recommended Reading section).

Cube method

The cube method is based on similar principles of training the three powerlifting lifts employing the same three main components as the conjugate method above: the dynamic method, the max effort method and the repetition method. However, the training sessions are arranged in such a way that no two lifts are trained heavy in the same week.

Lift	Monday	Wednesday	Friday	Sunday
Squat	Max effort	Dynamic effort	Repetition work	Mild cardio and core training
Bench	Dynamic effort	Repetition work	Max effort	
Deadlift	Repetition work	Max effort	Dynamic effort	

Max effort sets should be trained to technical failure only. Once the main lifts have been completed select a couple of accessory lifts to train with light weights and high reps (15–20). A fourth day of light cardio and core body training can be added.

Reps in reserve (RIR) and rate of perceived exertion (RPE)

All the training programs and cycles have so far been discussed in terms of performing a specified number of reps, but there are other options that can be useful. Form breaks down as fatigue increases and the number to technically correct reps you perform is more important than the total number of reps you complete. Consequently, it can make sense to leave a few 'reps in the tank' also known as keeping some reps in reserve (RIR) and one way to do this is to train according to the principle of rate of perceived exertion (RPE). This is a subjective method of estimating how much more intensity and/or volume you can complete based upon the work already done in the current set, measured against a pre-determined scale. Essentially, you are constantly assessing your level of fatigue as you perform each rep and will aim to stop at a certain level of perceived exertion. Using a RPE scale can also be beneficial because on a particularly bad day you may not be able to hit your prescribed number of reps in a normal program, but you will always be able to hit a specified RPE.

There are various different iterations of the RPE scale and you should choose or create one, based on your own circumstances (an example is shown below). Studies have shown that experienced lifters are more accurate when deciding RPE at high intensities. This is because they are better able to understand their bodies and what they can handle, when compared to a novice lifter who may underplay the amount they can move for a certain number of reps.

RPE	Volume & intensity
10	Could not do more reps or load
9.5	Could not do more reps, could do slightly more load
9	Could do one more rep
8.5	Could definitely do one more rep, maybe two
8	Could do two more reps
7.5	Speed fairly quick like an easy opener
7	Could do three more reps
6	Fairly easy, like a warm-up weight
5	Too easy to count as a work set

Training to (technical) failure

You will no doubt hear of people (usually bodybuilders) training to failure or AMRAP (as many reps as possible) in order to develop muscle mass, but this is not a good idea for powerlifters, at least with regard to the main competition lifts. As has been stated previously, form breaks down as a result of fatigue, so training to failure will require completing the last few (and hardest) reps using poor technique, inviting all sorts of potential injuries as a consequence.

Moreover, if you train to failure in the gym and allow your technique to break down in order to squeeze out a final rep, then you are likely to apply the same poor form on the platform when trying to hit a new PB, which may of course result in getting red-lighted and a failed attempt. It is absolutely imperative that your lifting technique is impeccable at competition when you will be pushing out your heaviest lifts under extreme fatigue. Hence, a simple training goal should be to make all reps consistent, whether they be light warm-ups through to a heavy work set or a max single.

A better approach is to train to technical failure, whereby you stop the working set as soon as you feel your form starting to break down and do not include that last rep in your count of work reps. As the adage goes, *training to failure is training to fail*. You do not want to fail lifts on the platform, so do not do it in training either ... leave that for the bodybuilders!

You are now familiar with the concepts of manipulating different variables in order to impose different stresses that promote increased strength development. As noted throughout this book, everybody is different and this includes in how they respond to different training routines. This fact is reflected in the huge number of different training programs available to strength athletes. Just do an online search for "powerlifting programs" and you will be rewarded with a multitude of links to all sorts of different routines, including downloadable spreadsheets, where you can enter your own 1RM values and the spreadsheet will calculate what weights you need to lift and for how many reps in order to achieve a new predicted max. Look at a few different examples and consider how they might work for you based on your experience to date. The important thing at this point is that you keep progressing and you should now have sufficient knowledge and experience to make this happen. If you get stuck you can always resort to a specialist powerlifting coach to get you back on track.

Fatigue, deloads and plateaus

Fatigue and deloads have already been mentioned briefly under the various different training stages above. However, understanding these concepts becomes more important during the intermediate stage because the balancing act of inducing an adaptation (as often as possible) in order to get stronger faster, versus the need to manage fatigue becomes more complicated. In general, the more advanocd the lifter, the greater the fatigue from the stress that is sufficient to cause an adaptation. Again, regular deloads can be built in to your training program or you can add them in as and when you feel like they are needed.

As at the end of the novice stage, you will recognize the onset of a plateau because you will slow down before you stall completely. This early decline should be tested to determine whether it is the onset of a true plateau or whether it is due to some other factor such as poor sleep, poor nutrition or just having a bad day. Do not give up on your program straight away, but rather drop the weight to about 80% for a few deload sets then have a good rest and try the failed work set again next time you are scheduled to train that lift. Make sure you are well rested, well fed and fully focused on the job that needs to be done. If you still fail then it is likely you are hitting a true plateau and you will need to find a smart work around to get through it. If you just try and push through it by repeating the same weights session after session you will surely stall and impede your progress.

The best option is to incorporate small changes based on your recent training performance which will hopefully result in steady, long-term progress. If you make a small change and it works, then keep running with it. If it does not work then try a different small change. Operating in this manner (as opposed to switching to a completely different program) has the benefit of manipulating single variables at a time, which means it is easier to judge what helps (or does not help) drive your progress at that particular moment in time.

The point at which you have failed the lift as you entered the plateau will indicate which part of the ROM (range of motion) is your weakest part of the lift. For example, in the bench press it may be the lock-out towards the top or it may be getting the bar off your chest at the bottom. Training the accessory lifts that support the particular ROM weak point is likely to have a significant impact on improving this problematic element of the lift. Eventually though, a new weak link in the chain will appear and it will be time to find the next set of accessory exercises that will fix the new problem.

Train efficiently

As with competition day there are things you should do the day before you train in order to maximize your efficiency and effectiveness in the gym. You should have all your kit packed and ready to go the night beforehand and you should know exactly what your training plan for the day will be in terms of what lifts and accessories you will be performing, including reps, sets and weights to be lifted. Essentially, you should be able to pick up your bag, enter the gym and get straight down to business without any need to faff around. To this end, I keep a hand written diary with all my training schedules pre-planned according to the program I am following. If you wait until you get to the gym before you decide what to lift your progress will suffer. Just remember the principle of the 6Ps: *Proper Prior Preparation Prevents Poor Performance*.

Recover efficiently

Your strength does not increase in the gym. Training provides the stimulus, but the adaptive strength gains occur during the recovery phase between training sessions. There are a number of things you can do to help maximize your potential for recovery and adaptation during this period. The most important things to manage are sleep (try and get at least eight hours, which can include a nap throughout the day) and nutrition (remain hydrated and focus on healthy high-protein food choices). It is always a good idea to avoid drugs (including legal ones such as alcohol and smoking) and unnecessary stress.

Common mistakes regardless of the training program

There are a number of common mistakes that many lifters make regardless of which program they decide to employ and all of these will impact on how effective your training will be. These include:

- Lifting with bad form (either from the outset or as a result of form creep as the weight intensity increases).
- Setting your starting weights too high (ease yourself into a new program – don't worry, the weights will get heavy soon enough!).
- Applying inappropriate increments as you progress (either too light to initiate an adaptive response or too heavy to complete the reps and sets with good form).

- Altering an existing program that has a proven track record in other lifters (trust the process, though of course there is no one-size-fits-all but any changes need to be fully justified and monitored accordingly).
- Adding in too much accessory work (will increase cumulative fatigue).
- Missing training sessions (for obvious reasons).
- Rushing through training sessions (will lead to bad form and increased risk of injury).
- Lack of focus on recovery (this is when your body adapts and strength gains are made).
- Inappropriate nutrition (lifting heavy is hungry work!).

Dealing with aches and pains

Unfortunately, the odd ache and pain must be accepted as part of the process and you will soon be able to differentiate between the two. Aches can be considered benign and are normally just an indication that you have started using muscles that have been relatively unused to moving heavy loads. Clearly then you are likely to experience this during the initial stages of your training, but once your body gets used to the process they will mostly become a thing of the past. Furthermore, you will probably start to develop a kind of love-hate relationship with aches because they tend to signify that you have worked very hard physically and you will be able to expect decent adaptation through recovery. Such aches are often referred to as DOMS (delayed onset muscle soreness).

Although there are some who advocate that a post-training sauna can assist with muscle recovery there is no unequivocal evidence of this. Nonetheless, they can be relaxing and re-invigorate you, so give it a try if your gym has one, but limit the time inside to around 20 minutes and make sure you re-hydrate yourself afterwards. There is also some suggestion that a post-training massage can alleviate the effects of DOMS, but again, the evidence is not particularly conclusive.

Pain, on the other hand, is a different matter and can occur as the result of several reasons, though you are more likely to suffer from pain as a result of joint-bashing cardio exercises than you are from strength training. Using poor technique or having inadequate range of motion before you start, may lead to pain, especially in the elbows, knees, hips or shoulders. This may manifest as sharp pains whilst training or stiffness outside of the gym, e.g. your shoulders might start hurting and seizing up while you are sleeping. If you start to experience this then make sure you employ some flexibility and mobility exercises for the relevant joints before you start the main work sets of your training session. You will need to scrutinize your technique (which you should be doing constantly anyway) to ensure that it is correct and maybe modify your grip or foot position in order to accommodate your particular biomechanical preferences.

At some point during your training you are bound to tweak a muscle or two. This will manifest itself as a sharp pain when you move in a particular way, rather than a dull and consistent ache, as per DOMS above. Again, this may result from poor technique or as a result of not warming up properly. If you feel an injury happen during a training session, stop what you are doing and re-rack the bar immediately. Do not squeeze out another rep or try to finish your set as you have potentially more to lose than gain by doing so. The same goes for incurring an injury during a competition. It is safer for everybody (especially you) if you withdraw, rather than continue and compound the problem or risk causing injury to spotters. I had to withdraw from the 2022 North West Championships after unracking my first squat attempt. A lower back injury from which I thought I had recovered remanifested itself as I walked out of the squat rack. I had no option but to return the bar to the rack, leave the platform and withdraw from the competition.

Following an injury you will need to start a rehabilitation program (see the book *Rebuilding Milo* in the reading list) and train around the pain, but not through it. Trying to train through the pain is likely to make matters much worse – the old adage of '*no pain, no gain*' does not count here! Training around the pain refers to conducting exercises that support certain elements of the various lifts, but which do not directly utilize the painful muscles under extreme loads, though I am an advocate for keeping the damaged muscles moving. This will allow you to continue to make some progress as the damage heals. It is beneficial to massage painful muscles, so I always carry a muscle roller stick and a tennis ball in my gym bag. Most gyms will have a foam roller lying around somewhere and I also find a trigger point massage tool useful for pinpointing problematic areas in difficult to reach places. Recovery may take one week or it may take a lot longer depending on where the damage is and how bad it is. Hence, the best thing to do is concentrate on correct form at all times in order to reduce the likelihood of such injuries.

Certainly, you must not stop training completely on account of an isolated muscle pain because this will more than likely derail your progress totally and may also result in you quitting entirely! If you speak to most powerlifters, especially Masters lifters, you will probably find they are usually walking around with a whole suit of minor injuries and niggling pains. Of course, in the unlikely event of severe pain you may need to seek medical advice before continuing with your training but try and find a doctor who fully understands the benefits of heavy lifting.

A serious knock-back can shatter your confidence. Your mind will certainly play tricks on you after you receive an injury and this may lead to your giving up lifting all together. Do not let this happen! If you do a quick internet search you will come across many stories of powerlifters (and other strength athletes) who have sustained serious injuries (no doubt considerably worse than the one afflicting you), but who have all made a remarkable comeback through sheer will and determination. As with most personal attributes resilience can be developed over time, but only if you do not give up at the first sign of trouble!

Of course, we are all afraid of major injuries incurred while lifting, but it is much more likely you will hurt yourself as a result of a simple accident caused by a lack of concentration. In my experience, the most common injuries concern fingers and toes/feet. Fingers can be crushed returning dumbbells to racks, or getting them trapped between or under weight plates. A common cause of foot injury is removing a large plate from a squat bar without noticing a smaller (1.25 or 2.5 kg) plate also on the bar – as you remove the large plate the small plate drops to the floor and usually lands on your foot or toes. Such events can cause serious pain and damage which can curtail your training for a significant period of time.

Warming up

Doing any exercise, but especially lifting heavy weights, with stiff and inflexible muscles increases the risk of incurring an injury and bringing your training session to a premature halt. The consequences of not warming up properly can last for days or even longer! Warming up properly will increase your core temperature and make your muscles (and other associated soft tissues) more pliable. It will also increase the range of motion around your joints, and will facilitate explosive movements, whilst minimizing the risk of developing painful conditions such as tendonitis (e.g. tennis elbow).

There are all sorts of different things you can do to warm-up, from static or dynamic stretching (some authorities suggest leaving stretching until the end of your training session), using a foam roller or resistance bands, through to conducting your main lifts with an empty bar. In choosing how to warm-up properly you will need to select exercises that target the muscles and joints you will be using in the main lifts that day. However, your time in the gym is valuable, so do not waste the majority of it warming up!

Warming up with an empty bar, followed by light increments may be sufficient for some people, but make sure you do not fatigue yourself before you get to your main work sets. Your warm-up can be structured according to the number of reps planned for your work sets. For example, a work set of 6–8 reps will represent a relatively low percentage of your 1RM, so you can jump straight on to your first work set following a final warm-up set of four reps (e.g. 10, 6, 4, work set). Conversely, a work set of 1–3 reps will be very close to the top end of your 1RM, so you will need a couple of extra single rep sets to work up to it (e.g. 10, 6, 4, 2, 1, 1, work set). A work set of 4–5 reps sits somewhere in the middle, so you will probably just require one heavy single at the end of your warm-up (e.g. 10, 6, 4, 2, 1, work set).

If you find you are having difficulty getting into the correct position to conduct a particular lift, then this is probably an indication that you have limited range of motion around a particular joint. For example, if you have difficulty setting up under the bar for the squat, you may have shoulder mobility issues and so your warm-up should focus on resolving this. Similarly, if you are unable to squat deep enough then the mobility problems may be associated with the hips or ankles and you should pay special attention to these regions.

Setting goals

Training goals and competition goals are very different. Training goals can be either short-, medium- or long-term and result from consistent training over an extended period of time. Sometimes you will have good training days and sometimes you will have bad training days, but your progress towards your goals will continue regardless so long as you remain consistent and keep turning up. The goals may of course relate to hitting certain numbers at competition. However, hitting those numbers on competition day can be an entirely different matter as the time frame in which to achieve what you set out to do is limited to just a matter of hours. Consequently, you need a different and highly flexible approach to competition goals and these are discussed separately under *Setting your competition goals* in the Competitive Powerlifting chapter.

For most people the deadlift will be their strongest lift, followed by the squat, with the bench press being their weakest lift. The table below shows some realistic short- and long-term goals for a newbie lifter (bw = body weight).

Lift	Goal 1	Goal 2	Goal 3	Goal 4
Deadlift	1.0× bw	1.5× bw	1.75× bw	2.0× bw
Squat	0.75× bw	1.0× bw	1.25× bw	1.5× bw
Bench press	0.5× bw	0.75× bw	1.0× bw	+1.0× bw

At the outset, goal 1 will be your first short-term goal and goal 4 will be your first long-term goal, with goals 2 and 3 being intermediate-term goals. As you progress, the first intermediate-term goal becomes your next short-term goal and new longer term goals can be set. So, by the time you have reached goal 3, your initial long-term goal is now your next short-term goal and by now you should have set new goals 5 and possibly also 6. These goals can be achieved by following the progressive overload training method, which involves adding slight increments to the bar each time you train, assuming you have managed to hit the prescribed number of sets and reps in the previous session.

Obviously, your initial strength and mobility when you start out will determine how quickly you reach your first goal. People also vary in how they respond to the training stimulus and so some will maker quicker progress than others, but all newbie lifters should make relatively good and rapid gains. Indeed, the above table is indicative only and you may even want to reduce your first short-term goal. Your first short-term goal should be readily achievable without too much effort and the degree of difficulty required to reach subsequent goals can be increased once you have developed more confidence and motivation as a result of achieving earlier goals.

The Powerlifting Mindset

In many respects, powerlifting is a much a mental sport as it is a physical one and it is important that you do not underestimate the power of your mind for working towards achieving your goals or for conspiring against them. It can be your greatest ally or your worst enemy. A positive feedback loop develops whereby a high degree of mental strength will allow you to focus and push harder to develop greater physical strength, which in turn feeds back to increase your mental fortitude (both inside the gym and in normal daily life), and so the cycle continues ... and hopefully repeats itself.

There is a broad range of mindset issues that need to be dealt with or overcome in order to train and compete effectively. You need to be able to commit yourself, you need determination, focus and drive, you need patience, you need to self-appraise critically, you need to accept criticism from others, you need to have confidence in yourself and be able to perform under pressure, you need to deal with failure in both the immediate and longer terms, whilst at the same time being able to manage self-doubt.

If you compete you will also most likely need nutritional discipline in order to make your weight class. You will want results and these cannot be obtained in the presence of excuses, so you will need to make yourself fully accountable to yourself. You will need good problem-solving skills in order to overcome obstacles in your training program or in daily life, which may have the potential to impact on your training routine. All in all, you need to have a very positive, progressive and strong mindset.

If this all sounds too much, you can use a powerlifting coach who can help carry some of this load and help keep you accountable, but at the end of the day it is you who will be lifting the iron. There are numerous books written on sports performance psychology and mindset, so only a few pertinent examples are briefly discussed here and elsewhere in the text.

Commitment to training

Powerlifting training is all about consistent progression over a long period of time. This is relatively easy to do when you first start out because newbie lifters make relatively rapid progression in terms of both technique and strength gains, which can continue for several months. However, at some point this progression will start to plateau off as you reach your physical limits in this initial training phase. At this point the training will become physically harder and your mind will start interfering by filling you with self-doubt and making you worry about killing yourself under a heavy weight or injuring yourself so badly that you will never walk again. It is at this point that staying in bed can seem more appealing than getting up on a cold wet morning and going to the gym. Do not let this happen! All you need to do is modify your training program accordingly in order to stimulate and stress your body in a different way than what you have been doing.

You need to commit to training at least three times per week, every week. If you start missing the odd session here and there it will affect your strength gains and it will not be long before you start skipping two sessions per week and then several weeks at a time. You will have wasted your time! Understanding the difference between motivation and commitment is all important. There will be times when your motivation to train disappears and at this point somebody who relies solely on motivation will skip a session. However, if you have decided to commit yourself to the process then you will still go and train regardless of your motivational status on any given day.

COVID lockdowns

One of the most significant life events to impact on powerlifters in recent memory was the forced gym closures during the COVID lockdown in 2020/2021. On the day these were announced (Friday 20 March) I had no options for training outside of my regular gym, but by the end of the following day I had acquired a barbell and 135kg of bumper plates and constructed some blocks to lift off. Many others had the same idea and there was a massive upsurge in online gym equipment sales. Many stores were sold out in hours and certainly within a matter of just a few days. Social media was full of people looking to get hold of whatever kit might still be available and many sellers hiked up their prices considerably and/or were only accepting minimum orders of £1000 due to the exceptionally high demand.

After three and a half weeks of lockdown I'd had enough of being only able to floor press off my home-made blocks, so built my own bench. This opened up a whole new range of training options for my garden workouts, but it was not possible to go heavy without a rack to support the bar and lift off from, so I also built a power rack complete with safety bars, rack pins, band and pull up attachments. Both were of exceptionally solid construction and served me well. Eventually, the gyms re-opened after four months and I had managed to maintain much of my strength. On November 1st it was announced that the entire country would be plunged back into a full lockdown (which again lasted several months) and we were given only a matter of days to prepare for this. It would be no fun whatsoever training outside at this time of year, so I needed an indoor solution quickly. Most online stores had still not managed to restock their lines that they had sold out of during the first lockdown, however, I managed to find a reasonably priced half-rack that would fit in a spare room and which arrived the day before the lockdown.

Eventually, so-called 'Freedom Day' happened in the UK on 19th July and opened up the possibility for competitions, so I registered for two in August, The first of was the British Bench press Championships 2021, held at Moulton College on 7 August, followed by the North West Masters Championships. From chatting with people at these comps, it was evident that the lockdowns had quite a profound effect on a number of lifters. Many had either put on, or lost, considerable amounts of weight or had lost all motivation to train, either due to the lack of available facilities and/or the lack of competitions on which to focus. Consequently, the competitions that did happen were not particularly well attended, despite the organizers making extra allowances, such as qualifying totals dating back to 2019, including qualifying in a different weight class to that being entered in the upcoming comp. For example, there were only around 70 lifters at the 2021 British Bench Championships, whereas there were approximately 150 competitors at this event in 2020 just before the first lockdown. The same was true for other competitions and was also reflected in the membership of British Powerlifting, which was down more than 50% on the previous year (approximately 1850 compared with 4600).

From the outset until the end of the lockdown my focus and commitment to training was unwavering. As each new obstacle arose I sought and affected a work-around solution. Had I not been so committed to training, I would probably have given up at some point during the process.

Trust in the program

As already mentioned, in the early stages of training newbie gains are significant and frequent. However, once you start to plateau you (or your coach) will need to adjust your program in order to keep them coming, but from this point onwards the strength gains tend to be smaller and less frequent. This, in and of itself, is enough to deter some would-be powerlifters. The initial strategy once a plateau has been reached is usually to drop the amount of weight lifted (the intensity) and to lift it for more reps. In other words, you switch from a strength training block to a volume (hypertrophy) block as a means for building more muscle and a new basis for a subsequent strength training block. Building muscle is a slow process and you will need to increase your calorie intake and make sure you get enough sleep in order to accommodate it. Remember, muscles grow in the bedroom, not in the gym, the gym just supplies the stimulus for growth!

Alternatively, you may employ an established program based upon various different percentages of your maximum lifts (e.g. 5-3-1). In either case you are imposing a new and different training stimulus on your body and it may take a while for this to yield new strength gains. You need to trust the process, which can be easier said than done when your mind keeps telling you that you are most probably losing strength and you should check your 1 rep max just to see what's going on ... or even worse, to hop from one new program to another and then another without allowing sufficient time for any of them to produce results. The name of the game here is patience, which is something that is often lacking in younger lifters these days, mainly due to the immediacy of the modern world in which we currently live.

Performing under pressure

It cannot be overemphasized how different competition lifting is to lifting during training and there are several elements of your mental approach to competition lifts that are worthy of discussion here. Competitions are great fun and an opportunity to make new friends and catch up with others who you may have not seen for some time, but you must not let this distract you from your main purpose of being there. You need to have your game face on before you even arrive at the event and you must maintain your focus until after your last lift of the competition. In addition to actually performing the lifts there is a lot of other stuff to manage over the course of the event and if you find yourself not doing the right thing in the right place at the right time, you might disadvantage yourself (e.g. by having to rush your warm-ups, being late to the platform, missing a lift, forgetting to submit an attempt slip, etc.) and disturb your focus and psyche by fretting over it. It is for this reason that a coach or handler is recommended for your first few competitions, but once you have a few events under your belt it is reasonably easy to manage everything by yourself.

As with anything, the more you do something the better and more confident you will become at it. At least this is usually the case, although there are some people who find it difficult to overcome stage fright regardless of their degree of experience. The first time you do something will (most likely) be the time at which you experience the greatest degree of nerves and so it is your first competition that is likely to present the greatest test of your resolve. Fortunately, there are several different levels of competitions designed for new, inexperienced lifters (and these are discussed further elsewhere), but it would make sense to start off at one of these where most of the other lifters are in the same situation as yourself (and the judges tend to be more lenient and helpful if you find yourself doing something incorrectly). I can guarantee that the first time you are called to the platform your nerves will kick in and your legs will probably start to feel week (not particularly good for your first ever competitive squat!). You must just ignore this and get on with it, but this is the reason why it is imperative that you select easy weights for your opening lifts (if you can perform 140kg easily for reps in the gym, then select 120kg maximum as your opener.

It is important to psyche yourself up for your lifts and there are several different options for doing this. The first is to use the above-mentioned (nervous) adrenalin that makes your legs feel like jelly and gives you butterflies in the stomach and channel that energy to work for you rather than against you. Consider it as lifting juice flowing through your veins and visualize it as such. Tell yourself in your mind, very firmly, "This is my lifting juice coursing through my body and it helps me lift HEAVY shit!"

Different lifters will vary in how they prefer to prepare themselves mentally at competition and this may include variation in how an individual lifter prepares for the different lifts. There is an inverse relationship between the level of skill involved in a lift and the degree of arousal necessary to complete it successfully. This means that the level of arousal needs to be low for high-skill-level lifts (e.g. squat and bench press), otherwise it may lead to breakdown in technique, whereas arousal can be high for low-skill-level lifts (e.g. deadlift). This is why you will often see more passion from lifters during their deadlift set up than you will for the other two lifts.

Some people prefer a calm and internally focused approach, whereas at the other end of the spectrum other lifters will wind themselves up almost into a state of frenzy. You will see some people listening to (usually very loud and angry) music

183

Opposite page: The author lifting competition specification plates for the very first time. This was at a charity event in Manchester, 2017 and boy did I get a surprise! I attempted a weight that I could lift relatively easily in the gym, but up until this point I had only used bumper plates, including in the warm-up at this event. Lifting thinner, steel plates is quite different as they come off the ground in a different way and feel significantly heavier! If possible, make sure you experience lifting with competition plates BEFORE your first comp! Image credit LD.

just before their lift as they wait to be called to the platform, removing their head-phones at the very last moment. Other lifters use smelling salts (the rules state that these should not be visible to the public) and although they may heighten your awareness momentarily, along with burning your eyes and the inside of your nose, ammonia inhalants do not have any performance enhancing effects at the neuro-muscular level. Some lifters will have their coach slap them very hard on the back, head or even in the face. Others psyche themselves up to the point where they scream at the bar as they approach it and/or give it a good firm shake before they begin their set up proper.

Experiment early on and do whatever works for you, but make sure you remain in control. If you hype yourself up too much it might impact on the focus you need to perform the lift to competition technical standard, including following the commands from the referee. You need to find your optimal state of arousal for each of the lifts. As you become more experienced there is a lower chance that a higher state of arousal will impair your ability to perform the lift with technical proficiency, so your optimal state of arousal can be expected to increase as your lifting career progresses.

Another tip in the lead up to your first competition is to employ some purposeful practice in your training. We are all creatures of habit and this is not a bad thing. I for one am certainly a victim of this! I have my favourite squat rack, my favourite bar, my favourite spotter and I always train in the same gym at the same time of day. With purposeful practice, the idea is to get out of your comfort zone by making your training harder in some way and this may be as simple as changing the variables mentioned above. Certainly, when you step on the platform for the first time everything will seem very different indeed, so the more you vary your training set-up in the run up to your first competition then the less of an impact this will have and so will be of benefit, particularly if you are of a nervous disposition.

As an example, the first time I competed was at a charity deadlift event. All my training up until the competition had employed thick rubber bumper plates. Even the warm-up at the comp had bumpers, with the single set of competition specification plates reserved for the platform. And so it was that the first time I ever lifted with competition specification plates was my first competitive deadlift opener … and boy did I get a surprise! The thin steel plates come off the ground very differently to the thicker rubber plates. The former all come up together whereas the latter tend to gradually peel off the floor from the inside outwards. I was not

prepared for this and the weight felt considerably heavier than I expected and what should have been an easy pull turned out to be a bit more of a struggle and this got me rather flustered for my subsequent attempts.

The take home message here: If you do not train with competition spec plates, racks and benches, I would VERY strongly advise you to organize a day pass to a gym that does have them. This will allow you to get a feel for the difference and not end up with a similar nasty surprise the first time you step on the platform. Make sure you use them to train all three of the lifts you will be doing.

Also, try and avoid training in front of a mirror (or directly in front of a wall) all the time. It is useful to do so occasionally just to check your form, squat depth etc., but there will be no mirror on the platform and you will need to judge your lifts solely by how they feel. Once you have done a few competitions the need to mix your training up as suggested above is not as important because you will already know from experience what to expect on the platform.

Chalking up and getting in the zone prior to stepping on the platform at the North West Masters Championships, 2022.

Platform PB mindset

The last point at which you want your mind to start messing with your head is just before you walk on to the platform. Assuming you understand and respect your physical limits and this has been taken into account in your attempt selection plan there should be nothing to worry about with regard to your openers or the subsequent attempts. You need to be able to empty your mind of all superfluous thoughts and focus only on completing the lift. Going through the process of tightening your wrist wraps and chalking your hands (both of which need to be done before you start walking towards the platform) provides a perfect cue and opportunity to focus in on the work to be done over the next 30 seconds or so. One trick is to create a lifting mantra that gets you in the zone. This should not be a technical coaching cue, but something more relevant to the lift as a whole and most importantly, it must be something that resonates with you. It should consist of one to three words that you can repeat over and over in your mind as you access the platform and set up at the bar. As well as helping to generate focus this also blocks unwanted thoughts that will hinder your concentration. You can see some examples in the visualization examples given below. Do not simply copy these, choose words or phrases carefully and make sure they work for you. Do not wait for the competition before you use them. Practice them whilst training heavy sets and singles in the gym.

Visualizing (internal imagery) the lifts

The more you do something, the better you become at it. If you have already accomplished a task many times over in your mind's eye, then you are more likely to be able to effectively perform the same task in the physical realm. Many elite athletes use visualization techniques for training and to gain a competitive edge at competition. Indeed, research has shown that using internal imagery during training and competition improves performance more than relying on psyching yourself up just before you compete. However, using the technique effectively requires much more than just visualization of a process. You need to employ all your senses, as you would experience them, as you mentally run through the process of the lift from start to finish. This technique cultivates a heightened state of mental awareness, which is known to boost confidence and enhance performance. Using this technique, you can help train your heavy lifts every day and you don't even need to visit the gym to do it. Watching recordings of your lifts will help you prepare your internal imagery protocol.

Visualizing the squat

I am waiting at the entrance to the platform, hands chalked, mind cleared, focus on, wrist wraps nice and tight, feeling the energy coursing through my entire body, muscles twitching, ready to go, hips and shoulders loosening up, fingers wiggling. Some decent sniffs to clear the sinuses followed by a deep breath. I've got this! I hear the command, "The bar is loaded", and the usher in front of me waves me forward. I quickly flick the buckle to close my belt and take a deep belly breath to brace into it as I stride confidently and aggressively towards the platform all muscles now nice and tight. I hear clapping and some shouting. My jaw is clenched. I can see the crowd in my peripheral vision, but I take no notice as my eyes are fixed on the centre of the bar. I step on the platform and approach the bar directly from behind the centre of it. As I approach the bar I stare at it, "It's my bar, It's my bar, It's my bar!" I stop in front of the bar and place both hands on it, first the left, then the right, no rush, turning my head slightly to make sure I am setting up both hands in the right place, thumbs over the top and the chalk creating a nice contact. Once happy with my position I give the bar a quick but firm shake to let it know I am there and that I am the boss. I duck my head under the bar and push myself forwards until I feel the bar pushing into my rear delts, just at that sweet spot where I like it, then I pull my elbows up and back slightly to wedge it in place, lats engaged. My body and the bar are now a single unit. I stamp my right foot firmly in place under the bar forming a perfect interface with the platform then move my left foot into place, drilling both feet into the floor, toes pointed outwards slightly and knowing that they are firmly planted approximately shoulder width apart. Another quick breath and brace, abs nice and tight with my core pushing outwards circumferentially into my belt creating perfect core stability. I straighten my legs to raise the bar from the stand and take two steps backwards, right then left, swing my hips outwards so my feet end up the same distance apart as when I started, making sure the bar is steady and my knees are locked-out straight, knee sleeves nice and tight. I curl my toes slightly to grip the floor and wait a moment for the referee's command, the weight of the bar on my back, locked in and feeling nice and light. I hear it, "Squat." Another final deep belly breath, brace, "EASY LIFT!" and then I break at the hips and knees to sit down into the squat, keep my chest up and with knees tracking out over the toes as I move down at a controlled pace to that sweet bounce spot just below parallel. I feel the recoil in my glutes and hamstrings and immediately fire the bar back upwards like a rocket, pushing up and backwards with my upper body and driving my legs downwards into the floor. Shouts of encouragement from the crowd. Once back to the start position, I lock my knees out and pause, still holding my breath, waiting for the final command. "Rack" and a wave of the arm. I pause a second longer then step forwards with my left foot to secure the bar back in the stand. Exhale. As I back out from under the bar I turn to check the score board and hear the MC, "Three white lights, it's a good lift for David!"

Visualizing the bench press

I am waiting at the entrance to the platform, hands chalked, mind cleared, focus on, wrist wraps nice and tight, no movement at the wrists, feeling the energy coursing through my entire body, arms and chest muscles twitching, ready to go, hips and shoulders loosening up, fingers wiggling. Some decent sniffs to clear the sinuses followed by a deep breath. I've got this! I hear the command, "The bar is loaded", and the usher in front of me waves me forward. I quickly flick the buckle to close my belt and take a deep belly breath to brace into it as I walk towards the platform all muscles now nice and tight. I hear clapping and some shouting. My jaw is clenched. I can see the crowd and spotters in my peripheral vision, but I take no notice as my eyes are fixed on the bench and bar. I step on the platform and approach the bench telling myself, "Tight, Tight, Tight!" I stop in front of the bench and turn to sit down on it. A quick glance over my right shoulder to check where the bar as I lean back onto the bench right hand gripping the bar, followed by the left, the chalk on my hands creating the best grip possible. I pull myself under until my eyes are just forwards of the bar and find a focal point on the ceiling, back arched. I tighten my grip on the bar, along with driving my shoulder and upper back muscles down and into the bench to form a perfect, solid base. Double check my grip with wrists straight and knuckles towards the ceiling, bend the bar, lats engaged. Feet planted firmly on the floor, toes curled to grip, pushing forwards to engage the leg drive. A quick shake of the bar to let it know I'm in charge then I straighten my arms to lift the bar out of the rack. Arms locked-out straight, I move the bar slowly forwards under perfect control to bring it to rest over my shoulders, still staring at my focal point on the ceiling. I stop and wait for the first command. I hear it, "Start". A momentary pause followed by a final belly breath and brace, then I start to lower the bar reasonably slowly and under perfect control, bringing my chest up to meet it. Everything is nice and tight as I touch the sweet spot and bring the bar to rest. It feels light. A moment later I hear the second command, "Press!" "FIRE IT UP!" and I launch the bar upwards and it flies back up nice and smoothly to the start position, as the crowd shouts out encouragement. I pause, arms locked-out, bar motionless, eyes still focused on the ceiling then hear the third command, "Rack! I pause a second longer then let my arms fall backwards to rack the bar back in the stand. Exhale. As I push myself out from under the bar and stand back up I check the score board and hear the MC, "Three white lights, it's a good lift for David!", followed by clapping from the crowd.

Visualizing the deadlift

I am waiting at the entrance to the platform, hands chalked, mind cleared, focus on, wrist wraps nice and tight, feeling the energy coursing through my entire body, arms and chest muscles twitching, ready to go, hips and shoulders loosening up, fingers wiggling. Some decent sniffs to clear the sinuses followed by a deep breath. I've got this! I hear the command, "The bar is loaded", and the usher in front of me waves me forward. I quickly flick the buckle to close my belt and take a deep belly breath to brace into it as I stride confidently and aggressively towards the platform all muscles now nice and tight. I hear clapping and some shouting. My jaw is clenched. I focus on the bar as I step on the platform repeating to myself, "Up, Up, Up!" I stop in front of the bar and position my right then left foot directly under it, perfectly positioned so the bar Is above my laces, thcn drill both feet into the ground, toes curled, creating a nice tight sensation in my quads and glutes. A deep belly breath and circumferential brace into my belt creating perfect core stability. Arms outstretched, lats engaged I lean down, slow and tight to grip the bar, right overhand first followed by left underhand, hips kept high, chest up and sitting backwards perfectly counterbalanced by the weight on the bar. My entire body is now tight and perfectly primed. Two firm pulls on the bar to wake it up, then a short breath and brace, "Press the floor, press the floor, press the floor!" and I leg press the floor, pulling the bar up easily in front of me, the crowd cheering me on. Once past my knees I drive my hips forwards "Up, up, up!" to complete the lift and lock the bar out at the top, where everything comes to a stop. The bar feels light and secure in my vice-like grip. I hear it, "Down!", from the referee and after a momentary pause I return the bar under full control back to the floor. It hits the ground with a satisfying thud. I stand back up, release my belt, turn to check the score board and hear the MC, "Three white lights, it's a good lift for David!", followed by clapping from the crowd.

Positive affirmation statements

Another useful technique to employ is the use of 'Positive Affirmation Statements'. These consist of short, potent statements that evoke a great deal of cognitive vision – literal, emotional and physical, and which can be used to foster an appropriate mindset. Your statements need to be precise, personal, written in the present tense and proactive. They can be focused on specific goals or more generally aimed at improving your performance. You need to think very carefully about constructing them, but once you have some experience it becomes relatively easy. You might want to post them on the door of your fridge or keep them somewhere more personal, but make sure you read them as often as you need to, which should be several times every day.

Positive affirmation statements have great potential and their power should not be underestimated when constructed and used correctly, even though you may feel a little self-conscious doing it at first. The fact that many elite athletes worldwide pay their personal motivation coaches large sums of money to generate such statements for them is clear evidence of this. In constructing them you will need to focus on positive statements rather than negative ones. A couple of examples that might relate to your nutrition and training program could be based along the lines of the following:

"I eat mainly high-quality foods because these provide the best fuel to drive my burning ambition in the gym" [positive] rather than, "I don't [negative] eat low quality foods because they don't [negative] provide the best fuel to drive my burning ambition in the gym."

"I constantly push myself further each time I train, resulting in no limits at the margin of my strength gains!"

When reading or speaking a positive affirmation statement or visualizing a lift it is important that you attach a significant element of emotion to the task. This could be imagining how you feel after pulling a 200 kg deadlift for the first time at competition or the success of going 9 for 9 at your first competition, or how proud you will feel standing on the podium for the first time having placed within the top three. Although these things have not yet happened you have to imagine them as if they have. Of course, you cannot lie to yourself, but although these events may not be true at the present time, they do represent the truth of desired outcomes. Certainly, you need to have confidence in yourself. After all, if you don't then who will? What we believe about ourselves can greatly affect our motivation, commitment and thus achievement and positive affirmation statements will come in useful for both your regular training and as part of your competition preparation.

Recommended Reading

There are plenty of blogs and other websites online with lots of useful information, but there are probably more with rather dubious offerings. Some of these come and go and do not necessarily represent a permanent record of accessible material. Hence, the reading list presented here is restricted to books that are available as traditional hard copies and which I have in my library. That is not to say that all books contain a wealth of reliable or even useful information. Indeed, in these days of self-publishing anybody can publish pretty much anything they want and in the preparation of this book I certainly came across a number of titles that fell short of my expectations. These titles are listed, but are marked here with an '*'.

Austin, D. & Mann, B. 2012. Powerlifting: The complete guide to technique, training, and competition. Human Kinetics, 212 pp. (My rating: 4-star)

Bolton, A. & Tsatsouline, P. 2022. Deadlift Dynamite: How to master the king of all strength exercises. StrongFirst, Inc., 175 pp. (My rating: 5-star)

Bryant, J. 2013. Bench Press: The science. JoshStrength, LLC (print-on-demand from Amazon), 121 pp. (My rating: 5-star)

Cianciola, C. 2020*. White Lights: The complete guide to your first powerlifting competition. Independently published, 114 pp. (My rating: 2-star)

Dellanave, D. 2013. Off The Floor: A manual for deadlift domination. Movement Fitness LLC, 127 pp. (My rating: 5-star)

Farncombe, L. 2022. Powerlifting Essentials. Grosvenor House Publishing Limited, 273 pp. (My rating: 3-star)

Gaglione, J. 2019*. Are You Ready to Compete. Independently published, 104 pp. (My rating: 1-star)

Henriques, T. 2014. All About Powerlifting: Everything you need to know to become stronger than ever. Mythos Publishing LLC, 486 pp. (My rating: 5-star)

Horschig, A. (with Sonthana, K. & Neff, T.) 2016. The Squat Bible: The ultimate guide to mastering the squat and finding your true strength. Squat University LLC (print-on-demand from Amazon), 127 pp. (My rating: 5-star)

Horschig, A. (with Sonthana, K.) 2021. Rebuilding Milo: The lifter's guide to fixing common injuries and building a strong foundation for enhancing performance. Victory Belt Publishing Inc., 400 pp. (My rating: 5-star)

Rippetoe, M. (with Bradford, S.) 2013. Starting Strength: Basic barbell training 3rd edition. The Aasgaard Company, 354 pp. (My rating: 5-star)

Rippetoe, M. & Baker, A. (with Bradford, S.) 2013. Practical Programming for Strength Training 3rd edition. The Aasgaard Company, 256 pp. (My rating: 5-star)

Simmons, L. 2009. Westside Barbell Squat and Deadlift Manual. Westside Barbell, 173 pp. (My rating: 5-star)

Simmons, L. 2011. Westside Barbell Bench Press Manual. Westside Barbell, 75 pp. (My rating: 5-star)

Sullivan, J.M. & Baker, A. 2016. The Barbell Prescription: Strength training for life after 40. The Aasgaard Company, 366 pp. (My rating: 5-star)

Zeolla, G.F. 2009. Starting and Progressing in Powerlifting: A comprehensive guide to the world's strongest sport. Lulu (print-on-demand from Amazon), 350 pp. (My rating: 3-star)

Printed in Great Britain
by Amazon

26590203R10110